"I believe many people suffering with eating disorders ask one question in common: 'If Recovery is Possible.' Seeking an answer is somehow easier than taking the necessary steps towards recovery! Over the last four years I have been a constant reader of Andrea Roe's work! Her writing and knowledge of Anorexia, Bulimia and other associated eating disorders are not only useful but also inspirational. Now with Andrea's second book *You Are Not Alone, Volume 2*, comes more inspirational readings; perfect for anyone suffering, recovering, or supporting someone with an eating disorder. I personally recommend Andrea Roe's work, as she has been a shining star in my own personal battle with Anorexia. Andrea, I am forever grateful to you for helping me find the right path on my road to recovery and reminding me that I am, in fact, **Not alone**!!"

– Kara Rimington, 20, from Australia

"This book is formed by truly inspirational 'artists' in their own right. Whether it be through a story, poem, visual art and/or music, *You Are Not Alone, Volume 2*, conveys its message throughout. This reassuring and comforting, 'real life' book reaches out to all those battling with, and in recovery from, an eating disorder, reminding them that there are other people in this world who are experiencing similar struggles and that they ARE NOT ALONE! Messages of joy shine throughout this book, providing its readers with inspiration and hope to begin/continue along their path to recovery – within it is written proof that eating disorders can and will be beaten, and that RECOVERY is POSSIBLE!"

– Stephanie, a student from North Wales, UK
is in strong recovery from an eating disorder

"It really touches my heart to know that I am not the only one fighting with my recovery from an eating disorder. *You Are Not Alone, Volume 2*, also gave me new hope and courage to keep on with my recovery. This book is a safe place you can come to when you are having an awful day, one of those days of fighting your eating disorder."

– Carly Cochran, 26, from Atlanta, Georgia
is in recovery from bulimia and binge eating

"*You Are Not Alone, Volume 2*, is another healing dose of comfort to all those struggling with eating disorders. It provides readers with inspiration and hope for recovery, even from the darkest places. The stories give readers a chance to relate to those who completely understand what it is like to fight an eating disorder every single day. Most importantly, this book sends out the message that eating disorders can be beaten and there is always support available to win the fight!"

– Danielle L. from PA is in recovery from eating disorders. She is learning to take things one day at a time and lives by the quote: "Just when the caterpillar thought the world was over... it became a butterfly."

"Andrea Roe's book, *You Are Not Alone, Volume 2*, is all inspiring, ever helping us to remember we are truly not alone in fighting whatever eating disorder we may struggle with or even have overcome. The book is a collection of different writings and art from people going through the same struggles. It gives me hope when I'm struggling, to hear how others were able to overcome their disorder. I know for me to hear from others' hearts who have gone through the same things and some who have overcome gives me hope, and I can pick up and read when I feel no one could possibly understand what I'm going through. Each writing is so precious, and there's something for everyone with some that will touch a very strong cord in you. As you flip through the pages, the more you can see how eating disorders, self-injury, etc. had tried to steal our voice that we had had all along. Once we are able to let go of whatever destructive pattern we have going on in our life, then the true healing begins. We may find joy we have never felt before, maybe actually just 'feel' for the first time or in a long time. The book also comes with a CD full of songs that are healing for the mind as well as the soul. I cannot say enough about how this book has helped me. It takes you through the ups and downs of individuals' struggles, but leaves you with a feeling of hope that not only are you not alone, but that there is light at the end of the tunnel. I think it would be awesome if there were more things out there like this, instead of things that are only going to hurt us or break us down (i.e. some magazines and television shows). All the best to everyone who contributed to make this book possible. My hope is everyone who picks this up and reads it will be blessed as I have, to continue in recovery or to get help if needed."

Jana R. L. Singer, Songwriter, Poetry Writer and Eating Disorder Advocate in her twenties from Alabama

"To know that others have struggled just as much, and that they cannot 'only' survive, but thrive and live a better life, is truly inspiring."

– Ashley P. from BC, Canada, is in recovery from anorexia.
She encourages others to find their voice,
and never give up on themselves

"This is a powerful collection of hopes, dreams, despair… and victories! They are all war stories, written by survivors. Thank you to Andrea and to each of the people who share their journeys with eating disorders. I started this book and read it all the way through. It reminded me of so many of the stages that I went through for thirty years, struggling with my eating disorder all alone. Back then, no one talked about it, and I had no role models to know that recovery is even possible! Well, now I am living proof that it is… and that life can be fabulous once you give up "Perfect!" If you or someone you know needs help, please speak up and tell someone. Don't settle for less than wonderful in your life. And don't give up five minutes before the miracle!"

Barbara Niven. Actress, Speaker, Coach, and
Eating Disorder Victim turned Warrior.
www.barbaraniven.com

"Andrea Roe's Volume 2 of *You Are Not Alone* and CD companion is a wonderful gift to everyone who has ever encountered, suffered, and recovered from an eating disorder. Through music, prose, and poetry this book and CD give all suffering with eating disorders inspiration and clarity to seek recovery. As a person who has struggled and recovered with an eating disorder, reading this book inspired me to become more aware of my own recovery. Andrea Roe's book gives many different voices to eating disorders and this book and CD will make those who are in the midst of struggling know 'They are not alone.' This book and CD should be in every treatment center."

– Stacey Prussman. Comedian, Actress,
Speaker, and Eating Disorder Advocate.
www.staceyprussman.com

"This book is an unflinching, no-holds-barred collection of the writings of women affected by eating disorders. I applaud the bravery and creativity of this compilation's contributors, as they describe their own journeys to happier, healthier lives."

– Jess Weiner. Self-Esteem Expert and Author of "A Very Hungry Girl," and "Life Doesn't Begin Five Pounds From Now" www.jessweiner.com

"Andrea is a voice of Hope for so many in the barren wilderness of the bondage of an eating disorder. Read these stories and be encouraged; you will see the journey of healing can be made! Andrea brings us all together so we remember we are not alone. There is Hope."

– Gregory L. Jantz, Ph.D., CEDS. Bestselling Author, Speaker, Therapist, and Founder of The Center for Counseling and Health Resources. www.aplaceofhope.com

You Are Not Alone

Volume 2

The Book of Companionship for Women with Eating Disorders

Recovery Is Possible!

A Collection of Personal Recovery Stories, Inspiring Poems, Song Lyrics, and Artwork

www.youarenotalonebook.com

Andrea Roe
with Shannon Cutts

Foreword by Anita Johnston, Ph.D.
Author of *Eating in the Light of the Moon*

The editor and contributors of this book do not dispense medical advice or prescribe any technique as a form of treatment for physical or emotional problems and therefore assumes no responsibility for your actions. If you have any concerns about your physical, mental, or emotional health, please contact your physician. In the event that you use any of the information in this book for yourself, the editor, the contributors, and the publisher assume no responsibility for your actions.

Library and Archives Canada Cataloguing in Publication

You are not alone : the book of companionship for women with eating disorders : a collection of personal recovery stories, inspiring poems, song lyrics, and artwork / [edited by] Andrea Roe ; with Shannon Cutts.

"Volume 2."
"Recovery is possible!"
Accompanied by a CD of songs.
ISBN 978-0-9783090-3-9

1. Eating disorders--Literary collections. 2. Bulimia patients' writings. 3. Anorexia nervosa patients' writings. 4. Eating disorders--Patients--Biography. I. Roe, Andrea II. Cutts, Shannon

RC552.E18Y67 2009 820.8'03561 C2009-902407-1

Cover artwork by Robin Maynard-Dobbs; Design by Brandon Roe
Cover and interior layout by Keylime Designs & Marketing Inc

April Dew Publishing Inc
202 - 15388 24 Ave.
Surrey, BC, V4A 2J2

Dedicated to all those suffering with eating disorders,
and the loved ones who support them.

Trigger Warning!

Please note that the contents of this book may trouble some people.

It contains detailed stories of people struggling with anorexia, bulimia, binge eating, sexual abuse, rape, physical and emotional abuse, mental disorders, self-harm and other addictions.

If you feel you may react negatively to the content, please do not continue reading.

Contents

Acknowledgements

I want to thank all the wonderful women whose voices are united within these pages. Thank you for sharing your stories, poems, artwork, and songs to making *You Are Not Alone, Volume 2* possible!

To my wonderful family in Austria – Mama, Papa, Stefan, and Klaudia: Thank you for your unconditional love, support, and belief in me. I am lucky and proud to have you as my family! Ich hab' euch lieb!

To my favourite Uncle Andi and my Aunt Beti: I'm looking forward to your next surprise visit!

Most of all, I want to thank my wonderful husband, Brandon, for his continuous support and endless patience, and for believing in me and my goals. You always saw something special in me, even during my darkest days. I am blessed to have you in my life! We have been through so much, and we are still here, together, stronger than ever! I love you so much!

To all my friends and family back home in Austria: Even though we do not see each other often anymore, I want you to know that your friendships mean a lot to me, and I am always looking forward to seeing you (and to receiving emails from you). I especially want to thank Barbara, Elke, and Martina.

I also want to thank all the wonderful women I met on my journey and who inspired me to get to where I am today. I especially want to thank Karen Cook for believing in me and supporting me, and for our long walks and talks. Many thanks also to Shannon Cutts for being an inspiration and working together with me on this project; and to Dr. Anita Johnston for your amazing work – I read your book, *Eating in the Light of the Moon* in German, during my struggles, and loved every page of it.

Foreword by Anita Johnston, Ph.D.

The Joy of Recovery

Public recognition of the magnitude of the problem of eating disorders has increased significantly since I began working in the field of eating disorders over twenty-five years ago. Back then, anorexia and bulimia were not exactly household names and the concept of disordered eating or emotional eating was rarely mentioned.

While I do not disagree that the path towards recovery can, at times, be a long and difficult one, I take issue with the idea that it is nothing but a grueling ordeal, one that is never over. I have had way too many experiences of being witness to the awe inspiring, **joyful** aspects of both the journey towards and the actualization of full recovery. In my experience, what an individual needs more than anything in order to begin this journey is **hope**. And whenever she encounters the inevitable stumbling blocks and frustrations along the way, she needs some sense of the meaning of her struggle, a glimpse of the joy of recovery, and a feeling that she is not alone.

Over the years, the media has spread the word about the proliferation of eating disorders in America and other westernized countries. Perhaps it is because of this that research has been funded, treatment programs have become more and more available, and a variety of treatment approaches have been successful. Many who have suffered from or continue to suffer from disordered eating have learned that 'you are not alone,' and through this enlightened discovery, hope is recognized and embraced as a reality and not simply as an unattainable dream.

The media, however, in an attempt to condense the complexities of eating disorders into nice, neat, sound bites, continues to create and perpetuate a belief that eating disorders are about food and weight and those who suffer are doomed to a life-long struggle of trying to be thin. By failing to seriously consider the deeper, "invisible" causes such as the hunger for emotional expression, the need for heartfelt communication, and the desire for nourishment of the soul, they are unable to bring forth a vision of the extraordinary opportunities for personal and spiritual growth inherent in the journey of recovery from eating disorders.

Granted, it is easier to depict eating disorders from the lowest common denominators – those more obvious physical expressions of disordered eating – binging, purging, or food restriction; weight loss or weight gain; or other compulsive behaviors or addictions. But what is lost in this approach is a failure to portray the magnificent exploration of heart and soul, wherein one finds the joy of recovery, both as a journey and a destination.

What is the joy of recovery?

It is the celebration of the whole of one's being, and the ability to laugh and cry at our imperfections. It is receiving the gifts of wisdom our most uncomfortable emotions can bring. It is full recognition of the uniqueness of each and every one of us so that comparing ourselves with another seems ridiculous. It is the ability to know, to really know, that small tiny steps are as grand as giant leaps. It is the exhilaration that comes with discovering who we are, rather than trying to be who others think we should be. It is in the honest expression of who we are and how we feel.

Where is the joy of recovery to be found?

It lies in the pages of this book where these amazing, courageous women offer up hope as they celebrate the truth and joy of their recovery. Here you will find stories, poems, artwork, and songs – both tender and fierce – written by those who have embarked on the journey towards freedom.

The joy of recovery is in discovering that **You Are Not Alone**. It is in being able to retrieve parts of our selves that had been lost or discarded. It is in observing our thoughts, feelings, and behaviors with curiosity instead of judgment. It is in learning to recognize and respond to our true hungers and our greatest hearts' desires. It is in discovering the meaning beneath the disordered eating. It is in the re-telling of our life stories from the vantage point of hero rather than victim.

The joy of recovery comes from the recognition that to be emotionally sensitive and highly intuitive is a gift, not a curse. It comes from honoring the Spirit of the Feminine, and from celebrating the feminine principle that exists within all of us – our emotions, our intuitions, and our desire for connection.

The joy of recovery is in rejoicing in the embodiment of that principle, and in becoming fully alive in the body of a woman.

Anita Johnston, Ph.D.

Author, *Eating in the Light of the Moon*
Director, Anorexia & Bulimia Center of Hawaii
Director, ‘Ai Pono Eating Disorders Programs
www.DrAnitaJohnston.com

Introduction by Andrea Roe

RECOVERY IS POSSIBLE

Recently, I was invited to share my story at an eating disorder awareness event. Now that I am recovered, it is my passion to spread the word of recovery and give others hope and support by sharing my story.

One of the girls at the event said that years ago her therapist told her that she would always have her eating disorder. She was told that she would never be able to get rid of it.

Now, years later, her situation has not improved – it has gotten worse. *Why?* Because she lost hope. She has given up on herself. She keeps saying to herself, "Why bother continuing the fight when there is no hope and no chance of getting better?"

"He who does not hope to win has already lost."
- Jose Joaquin Olmedo

Hope is what keeps us going. Without hope, there is no reason to continue. There is no reason to encourage yourself to get better.

The truth is, as soon as we start believing something, it becomes real. That is helpful when the belief is positive, but it can also be a major obstacle when you start believing something that does not help you. In this case, this woman started to believe this lie told to her by her therapist. She started to believe that she would never get better, and that's exactly what happened.

"Believe it can be done.
When you believe something can be done, really believe,
your mind will find the ways to do it.
Believing a solution paves the way to solution."
- David Joseph Schwartz

If you are in a similar situation, where you believe you cannot get better, now is the time to take action. Start surrounding yourself with people who do honestly believe you can get better. Draw your hope from them.

As soon as you start believing you can "divorce ED" (as eating disorder survivor and author Jenni Schaefer would say), you have taken the first step to breaking through to a new life full of wonder and beauty instead of pain and sadness.

That is what this book is all about. It is a collection of personal stories, poems, paintings, and songs of women who have survived not only eating disorders, but also other addictions, depression, social anxiety, self-harm, suicidal thoughts, mental disorders, emotional and physical abuse, sexual abuse and rape. It is a book of **hope**. A book to help you regain the belief that RECOVERY IS POSSIBLE!

I encourage you to read this book however you want to – from the beginning to the end, jumping around, or just randomly turning to a page and starting to read.

This is a book that you are invited to see as your own personal, portable support group. Whenever you are feeling blue, just start reading and listen to the music. Find in this book a source of inspiration, of hope, and acceptance. Use it as a tool to help you in your recovery.

We all came together for this project to unite our voices and speak out because we want YOU to know that **YOU ARE NOT ALONE!** We want you to know that no matter where you are right now this is not the end. You can get through this! Please do not give up on yourself! Keep on believing in yourself and continue to be strong!

Of course, it is important to remember that **recovery is something that happens within you** and no one else. No one can recover for you, and there is also no magic recovery pill.

It is a process. It takes time. It does not happen overnight. Your eating disorder started years before you first binged, purged, or starved yourself – and it will take time to overcome this disorder.

There is also no rule for how long it takes for someone to recover. We all have different stories to tell, different reasons why we developed our eating disorders, and we are all at different points in our lives. Please don't put too much pressure on yourself. Be gentle on yourself.

There will be setbacks....
But no matter what happens, *do not give up!*

I know how you feel. I know what it is like. I have been there! And I want you to know that this is not the end. Your life does NOT have to continue like this. There is a way out, there is help, there is hope, and recovery does exist. You can learn to love and enjoy your life again. Please stay strong and keep on believing in yourself!

Recovery really is possible!

Andrea

PS. Feel free to get in touch with me! Let me know how this book affected you; share your thoughts and stories with me. Feel free to contact me any time with questions or comments, or for some support at andrea@youarenotalonebook.com. I always welcome your e-mails!

PPS. For more information about the *You Are Not Alone* projects, please visit www.youarenotalonebook.com.

Believe in your dreams and they may come true;
believe in yourself and they will come true.
-Author Unknown

Inspiring Stories, Poems and Artwork

The Other Side

Looking Beyond the Mountain

By Jo

I remember long ago seeing recovery as this large, seemingly impassable, ominous mountain looming forebodingly in the distance.

It was dark, it was scary, and it stood for everything which I was not.

I did not feel capable of climbing the mountain, nor did I feel I had any inclination to try to climb it.

I was quite happy to camp out at the bottom. After all, if I had already sunk to the bottom, things couldn't get any worse, I couldn't sink further. The bottom felt like a safe and comfortable place to be.

For years I trundled along, feeling like the bottom was best. People had passed me on their way up and tried to talk me up and over the mountain. I had heard that the grass was greener on the other side, but down at the bottom, I couldn't see past the big black mountain and could not be lured from my place of seeming safety.

It seemed too treacherous, and too risky for a reward I couldn't even see. I was promised it was there, but without seeing it, I could not bring myself to believe that life existed beyond my spot at the bottom.

The years passed. A couple of times, I felt motivated to see what was on the other side of the mountain, but I would get a few steps up and remember how scared I was, and remind myself of all the reasons I had stayed at the bottom for so long in the first place until I convinced myself to turn around and head back down.

A couple of times I made it a quarter of the way up. Once I even made it half the way up. But then the path got slippery and I decided once again it felt safer to head back down. The terrain felt rocky and unfamiliar. I didn't think I could handle it. Surely the safest thing would be to go back down again rather than to take agonizingly slow steps forwards instead. Right?

I decided if I was going to make it up the mountain I could not go it alone. I was not entirely convinced I knew the way. Sometimes the path was not clear, sometimes the terrain was difficult, and sometimes the load I needed to carry just seemed too much. So I got myself a guide. It was scary to trust her; sometimes we would disagree on which path to take, sometimes I doubted her judgments because I allowed my fear to creep in, and sometimes I got angry with her when the terrain got harder and she encouraged me not to turn back.

But she helped lighten my load. She let me share it with her so that it was not such a burden as I climbed up and up. I found I didn't need some of the load anymore and so I left it behind. I found I could let go of some things without feeling the need to turn back down to the bottom. It made my journey to the top easier as well.

I did not do it all in one go. It was all in bite-sized chunks. Sometimes when I felt I could not go any further, I camped out, rested and talked things through, and went on when I felt ready to give it my all. My only rule was I could not give up and turn around.

The higher up the mountain I got, the more I persevered and the more determined I became to reach the top. I had heard a lot about it and I was desperate for the top to live up to all of my expectations. So I kept going. I kept finding little things which spurred me on upwards.

When I had lived down at the bottom, the top seemed dark, scary, looming, and ominous. Oddly, the higher I got, the smaller my view of the bottom became, the blacker and bleaker down below looked. It had not looked like that before. The bottom from this height looked kind of scary. All a matter of perspective – what you see depends on where you stand, so the saying goes right? I had often wondered how people saw the top as something achievable and desirable, when they could have settled for the bottom. Now I was slowly beginning to realize what I could become if I made it to the top.

After a long time traveling upwards, we eventually reached the top. My guide explained it was there she would leave me. Scared and worried, I asked her why she would leave me. She told me she needed to go back down to the bottom, to bring more people up to the top and to rally together those who were camping out along the path unsure of which direction to travel. She explained if I needed her, I would find her, but that she had faith that I could go onwards and upwards without her guiding me now.

She had worked with me building up my skills, I knew how to look after myself. She had taught me how to approach the different terrains I could possibly face in the future, and she had shown me the view from the top. I could look down and see "the other side" – the view which everyone had talked about.

But I never figured I would find myself there.

I looked down, and saw how far I had traveled up that mountain, and it was then that I finally knew that I did not want to turn around. I wanted to keep going.

My first view of the other side was amazingly beautiful and filled with potential.

That was when I realized my potential, and that most things are possible; even if at first they do not seem to be, they are achievable.

Now I am busy, building up the other side – my "other side" is as yet a work in progress – I am gradually developing it, finding out who I am, and choosing what direction I want to head in.

I urge you to see past the big ominous mountain. I urge you to step out of your comfort zone down at the bottom, I urge you to keep on traveling upwards and away from the ED.

You can reach your other side.

Persevere and you will make it.

Jo is twenty-five years old and lives in England. She struggled with eating disorders for ten years and is now recovered. If you want to get in touch with Jo, feel free to send an email to jo@youarenotalonebook.com

If You Ever Thought

If you ever thought, or still think, that you aren't ready for recovery,
the Time Is NOW.
You will never be readier.
If you ever thought, or still think, that recovery is too hard,
It is hard.
But LIVING at the end is easier.
If you ever thought, or still think, that you CAN'T do this,
You CAN.
You MUST.
If you ever thought, or still think, that it's about [food] + [numbers] + [behaviours] etc,
It's NOT.
It never will be.
If you ever thought, or still think, that you're not worthy or deserving,
You ARE worthy.
You ARE deserving.
We are ALL worthy and deserving.
If you ever thought, or still think, that you're not being heard,
Use your VOICE.
We're listening intently.
If you ever thought, or still think, that the ED gives you control,
It NEVER does.
Choosing to LIVE gives you control.
If you ever thought, or still think, that the ED is the solution,
It will NEVER be the solution.
It will always be the PROBLEM.
If you ever thought, or still think, that you can recover alone,
Reach Out.
You are NOT alone.
Don't bank on tomorrow being the day to begin recovery.

Only the PRESENT is guaranteed.
Don't delay.
Begin your journey NOW.
Step by step. You can get there. You will get there.
Now is the time to reclaim your life.
<u>So get living.</u>
Start fighting.

© Jo

What Defines Recovery For Me

Recovery is about being proud of who you are, about forgetting the voices that crave you to change yourself to be more like person x, y or z.

Recovery is about not wasting the person that you are here to be by trying to become someone or something that you're not.

Recovery is about waking up in the morning and not letting food be your first thought or worry.

Recovery is about waking up and smiling and realizing that you get to be you for another day.

Recovery is about learning to live again.

Recovery is about patience, appreciation, and co-operation.

Recovery is about realizing that your worst fears are your greatest feats, and once you've got past them, you can do whatever you please, you can get through anything.

Recovery is about perseverance, about not giving up when the going gets tough.

Recovery is about wanting to be YOU.

Who I Am: My Quest For Truth

By Liz Hardy

I do not even know how to begin this story. I am a twenty-two-year-old female. I am a college student. I am a friend. But my identity is not found in any of these things. For eight years, my identity was wrapped into an obsessive pursuit of thinness, the pursuit of a great panacea where my troubles would fade away because I was thin and nothing could get to me. Anorexia took over my life and affected every relationship I had, from my family, to my church, and my closest friends. I was a manipulator – one of the best – but it left me so lonely at the end of the day. I ran from love because I could not love the person I was and did not want to give anyone else that right.

Here is my truth: The media portrays thin girls to be happy, to be the ones with no real troubles, and says that thinness is something that should be sought after above all else. This happiness they allude to was far from the truth for me. As a child, I loved ballet dancing and I had always been weight conscious. To illustrate this point, my close family friend shared a memory of me as a child. She said to me, "Liz, you were about six and comparing the size of your thighs to the watermelon on the picnic table." I was only six and so scared of becoming "fat." I had equated body size with the amount of love that could be given.

I had turned most of my emotion inward after my parents divorced around this age. I started restricting and purging around the age of nine. I remember the first time my mother saw me throwing up. I was not ashamed of my actions; I was only angry that I had been caught. This was a struggle that I was wrapped up in for years. I spent my high school years hiding who I was from everyone. I spent a great deal of time trying to convince myself that I was not worthy of love or acceptance. I have scars on my body that could tell you a story from hurts, from failures, or from incomprehensible horrors.

On the outside, I was an over-achiever; I was active in clubs and always had a smile on my face for those that needed one. I am a strong Christian and one of my favorite verses is the one in which Samuel is told that God does not look at the appearance of a person, but at his or her heart. My heart was so wrapped up in past hurts that it controlled my life. My identity was found in shame.

Today, I am not ashamed. I have found my voice. My eating disorder does not own my life. I am at a healthy weight and have a healthy attitude, but the way my life changed was not through an ordinary route. Recovery became my way of life after being sexually assaulted. I had dabbled in recovery before. I had been gaining some weight, and tried to eat before this, but I was not serious in my commitment to recovery. I would sway back and forth with the level of my commitment changing according to the pressures life had placed on me in that moment. It took such a horrible experience to wake that little girl inside me up. That little girl had been sleeping so long! And now she was awake, she was scared, but she was ready to fight. Anorexia and bulimia were slowly killing me. I can see that in pictures from years past. If I let each bad experience I had gone through dictate how I would respond to this world, I would not be living – I would continue to be a shell of a person that could have hopes and dreams to live for. It was my choice.

I had been living a life of contradictions. I was continually presented with a choice for life, and I denied that right to myself. It took a callous disgusting act where my "NO" was not respected to wake me up. If anorexia had not destroyed me before, then paired with the rape I had experienced it certainly would. His words stole mine. My memories were clouded by his actions against me. This is not something I share lightly because it affected me to the core of my being just as my struggle with anorexia and bulimia had.

If I decided just to continue starving myself, I would be the only one to lose. Suddenly, I knew I had a choice to make when it came to who was defining my dignity. Would I continue to starve or binge and purge just to prove to my past that I would not be hurt again? Would I use anorexia as my way to respond to my rapist? What sense would that make? It was not my fault, but by continuing down that path that was what I would be telling myself. If there is blame to be cast, if there is one to be punished, it is not me. But for all of those years past, I had been punishing myself and it was now, oddly enough, time for me to celebrate.

How do you celebrate when you are a haunted woman? This is not a celebration where one picks up noisemakers as if it were New Year's Eve. For me, it was a quiet journey. I was afraid, but I was also determined. Anorexia, for me, was very self-focused. I had to search outside myself because my heart was so burdened by sin and by shame. My mind was worn out by too many tears from things that I would never want to name. I realized I needed to live for something greater. The greater, to me, is the unknown, the unknown of where the rest of these years could take me, but the first step was honesty. I had to be honest with myself and realize I deserved life just as much as anyone else.

When you first start to laugh, and to smile, it feels weird. You are so used to denying the simple pleasures in life to yourself that you have to constantly remind yourself that it is okay to be happy. To be sure, not every day is a walk in the park. There are some days where eating is the last thing you want to do, but you do it any way. Why? **You eat because you are winning.** You win over every lie that was spoken to you that your worth is only found in what you weigh. You win because when you are in recovery, you are fighting for something greater. You are fighting for the chance to live. You are living to be heard. And when you are heard, you are respected. **I am not my eating disorder, I am not shame, I am Liz and that is okay**.

Liz Hardy, a twenty-two-year old college student from the United States, dreams of becoming an English teacher. She is enjoying recovery after struggling with anorexia for eight years. She is a survivor, and that is her first and last thought every morning and night. If you want to get in touch with Liz, feel free to send an email to liz@youarenotalonebook.com

What I Am Made Of

Take each day at a time,
Making room for the life that I call mine.
The life I have yet to build.
The dreams so long that have been still,
And the dreams I have begun to dream.
One day.
Everyday.
Until…

Dreaming is seeing in my mind's eye.
What I want to be true.
Is it bad that what I want,
I hope will find its way to you?

I want happiness and peace,
Clarity and relief.
The storm is gone out to sea now
But question is what remains.

What remains can bring me peace and cause me harm.
What remains is a broken soul and tattered heart.
What remains is where I start.

Where I start
Is not where I end.
Where I start
Will be again and again.
Morning after the mourning.
Where I start is
Deep within my heart.

My heart lies open and broken once more.
My heart can be crafted and molded to fit.
But no, my heart, be still it for now.

For now, for now
Let my heart be open.

Be open to see.
Be open to show
Just what I am made of.

What I am made of
Is not from hurt, trauma, or abuse.
What I am made of is confusing love and peace.
Of yearning for peace that draws me to my knees
What I am made of
Makes me who I am.

What I am made of
I begin to find out
As I take each day anew.

© Liz Hardy

Speak

You forgot to feel.
And now, what you feel is all too real.
Too compassionate,
Calm, cool, collected, like water after the rain.

The emotion bubbles up
And boils over,

Like a pot left on the stove too long,
Allowing emotion to stew and never release
Until you evaporate again.

Up in the cloud of nothingness
Where you are looking down on yourself and wondering why,
Things seem easier up there in the great big sky.
Watch the world float by, unaware that you have taken a vacation,
That you have checked out,
Until you silently fall back down to the earth below.

Lying there still and undisturbed,
Your mind is at rest.
Your heart is at ease
Until you are awoken from this state of reverie

So tell me now what you feel.
Tell me what you see when things begin to turn.
Tell me what you know and what you have begun to learn.
Tell me how your mind still wanders.
Tell me how your heart still pounds.
Tell me how you silently listen for unknown sounds.

The phone rings.
Your senses are jarred.
It's him, you think.
Your body is tense.

Do not hold me to false pretenses.
What would you tell him?

You do not hold my love.
You do not have my allegiance.
You have my regret and my secret.

It's not so secret now.
Is that scary?

And at other times,
On another spectrum and plane,
my issues are not the same.
They do not lie in secret, they are not hidden.
Personalities clashing and the tug of war ensues.
My mind has split in two.
When I do not deal with life
I take it out on my food.
I take it out on myself.

My scars could tell you a story
Of pain too real and moments long lost.
I never really have to wonder what of the cost.
My life gone by,
The years a blur.
All I can remember now are things,
Things that can overwhelm or be overcome.
It is my choice, but sometimes,
Sometimes, it is still hard to find the voice.
To find the voice
Of one long silent.
To find the voice when others stay quiet.
To find the voice that is only my own.
To find the voice, my own unique tone.
And still I wonder if there is a story to tell.

I see the emotion that lies behind your eyes.
The fear, the burdens, the tears. You refuse to cry.
Who are you trying to defy?
You're only hurting yourself in the end.
The story is there to tell.
Until then, you are the one holding the pen.

Angel Wings

Black tears on the concrete.
Anger, frustration, fear: they meet here.
Pedestals are broken.
Angel wings close in to cover the lost, the vulnerable, the sacred,
All while harsh words are spoken

How do you go from silence,
Things left unsaid,
Perhaps silence perfect and endearing,
To a cacophony of noise?
Life.

Life meets on the sidewalk,
Where tears run dry
Looking into the sky.
Wishing on a star,
Change.

Black tears on the outside
Help heal what lies on the inside.

You tell me you want to hear.
You want to know.
You want to feel.

Can't you see I am just trying to heal?
All while these angel wings of mine are closed.

Divorcing Ed

Breaking up with your Eating Disorder

By Jenni Schaefer

As many as ten million women in America are married to the same guy. He is abusive, controlling, and manipulative. He makes promises he never keeps and has convinced these women that without him they are worthless.

This is definitely not the boy next door. He is not a policeman, doctor, attorney, or businessman. His job is to cause misery and distress in people's lives. His name is Ed.

Ed's name comes from the acronym E.D. – eating disorder. He can be anorexia, bulimia, binge-eating disorder, EDNOS (eating disorder not otherwise specified), or any combination of these.

Until I met psychotherapist Thom Rutledge*, my eyes were closed to Ed's existence in my life. Thom taught me to treat my eating disorder as a distinct being with unique thoughts and a personality separate from my own. I learned to divide my personality – Ed and Jenni. At first, I thought Thom was crazy when he suggested that I refer to my eating disorder by a man's name. But since he was a professional, and I was paying him to help me, I decided to give his approach a try. It worked. For the first time, I had hope that I just might be able to break free from the eating disorder that I did not even know I had.

I learned that having an eating disorder is like being in an abusive marriage. Just as a battered wife is scared to leave her husband, I was afraid to leave my eating disorder behind. It was all that I had ever known. I hid my battle scars from my eating disorder in the same way that women in abusive marriages frequently hide their bruises from friends and family. These women only find freedom when they decide to divorce their abusers. And that is how I was able to taste the same freedom in life. I quickly learned that I was only one of the millions of women trapped in an abusive marriage to Ed.

Some women may not be married to Ed, but they are definitely flirting with him. This includes the eighty percent of women in America who are dissatisfied with their appearance and the fifteen percent of young women who have substantially disordered eating attitudes and behaviors. These women recognize Ed in the desire to be thin, the experience of overeating, and the ongoing struggle to make healthy choices in regard to food and weight.

Many men know Ed today. In the United States, as many as one million males struggle with anorexia and bulimia. Eating disorders do not discriminate by gender, age, race, or economic class. And eating disorders come in every shape and size – every number on the scale.

Do you know Ed? I know him well.

Ed and I were together for over twenty years. I met Ed in dance class when I was four-years-old. He told me that I was too fat. As early as elementary school, he convinced me that I needed to start restricting what I ate. Ed accompanied me to birthday parties and went trick-or-treating with me on Halloween. Many years later Ed even tagged along with me to high school prom where he had fun comparing my body size to all of the other girls. "Whose dress is the smallest?" he wondered. Regardless of my dress size, Ed told me that I was too large, that I was not good enough.

In therapy, I learned that one way to distinguish myself from my eating disorder was to compare my values with Ed's. He valued thinness above all else. Only the number on the scale mattered. He decided whether a day was going to be good or bad depending on that number. On the opposite end, I valued many other things, including honesty, love, friends, and family. I knew that these things were all more important to me than my weight or dress size

It was not easy, but slowly, I learned how insane Ed really was, or more accurately, how insane he could make me. Ed could turn anything into a reason to binge, purge, or restrict. One day, I accidentally bumped into a car in a parking lot, and Ed's immediate response was, "Let's head to the closest fast food restaurant and binge." He reacted the same way when I forgot to mail in my rent check one month. If he really wanted to be helpful, he would have just said, "Jenni, mail in the check." But, no, with Ed, the solution to any problem involves food.

I finally began to break my ties with Ed when I stopped keeping secrets and started talking. Despite the rules I learned in elementary school, I actually found an appropriate use for tattling. Whenever Ed spoke to me, I told someone. Whenever I listened to Ed and actually did what he suggested, I revealed that too. I continued to report on Ed's behaviors, and my behaviors began to get better. I was recovering from my eating disorder, becoming stronger and healthier.

I learned that I had to put recovery first. Prior to my doing this, recovery was squeezed in at the bottom of my list of priorities, which included sending birthday cards to every person I had ever met in my life and going to every event that I was ever invited to attend (whether I wanted to or not). I often skipped therapy appointments in order to put my energy toward these kinds of people pleasing behaviors. Eventually, despite Ed's desires, I learned that getting better meant putting recovery above all else. Finally I began to discover what life could be like without Ed.

Getting better meant persistence, not perfection. It meant taking action. I practiced separating Ed's voice from mine. I gathered the strength and tools required to disagree with him. Even when I had trouble disagreeing with him, I learned that I could still disobey him. For instance, even if I believed Ed when he called me a "fat cow," I could still follow my food plan for the day. I could refuse to restrict despite the fact that I really believed I was a fat cow. I could always disobey. (For the record, Ed was never right about the fat cow thing.)

I fell down many times on my journey to full recovery. Each time I fell, I would reach out for help. My wonderful support team of friends in recovery, family members, and health care professionals always picked me up. They got really tired at some points, and I was exhausted, but I always stood back up again. That is why I am recovered from my eating disorder today. That is why I am living a life I never imagined possible – an amazing life woven with passion, balance, and dreams for the future.

My hope is that other women and men will find recovery from their eating disorders. The first step is simply awareness. After we realize that Ed exists, we can take steps to change. We can become less critical of our own body and of other people's bodies. And maybe other people will adopt our new attitude and behavior. We can focus on what our body does instead of what it looks like, and concentrate on healthy eating and exercise habits. We can begin to examine how culture has affected our own body image and self worth, and we can spread the message that weight and appearance are not the most crucial aspects of our identity. If we do all of these things, in the years to come, we just might see an increase in the divorce rate in this country (from Ed, of course).

Jenni Schaefer is a singer/songwriter, speaker, and the author of *Life Without Ed* (McGraw-Hill) and *Goodbye Ed, Hello Me* (McGraw Hill, September 2009). Appointed to the Ambassador Council of the National Eating Disorders Association (NEDA), she is a regular guest on national radio and television. For more information, visit www.jennischaefer.com

*For more information about Thom Rutledge, visit www.thomrutledge.com

Life with an Eating Disorder

My Struggle and Victory over Bulimia

By Lori Henry

Bulimia did not begin for me on a specific date or even a specific year. What seemed to hit me suddenly had taken years to develop and more to understand.

Nothing has affected me so deeply, hurt me so severely, or engulfed me so wholly. An eating disorder was my act of survival. I developed bulimia to alleviate the pain and confusion of being a sensitive person. Controlling food helped to numb the overwhelming sensations that bore down on me from all directions; I felt lost in a whirlwind of emotions I could not even identify.

Food became the easiest way to ease the harshness of the world. So many conflicting thoughts and feelings were surging through me that I concentrated on food to block out what I did not understand.

I was slowly building walls of protection and layers of caution around myself, but no amount of armour could shield me from my own pain. I spent my years in high school with a dead spirit and a fake smile on my face. All I cared about was the number on the scale and my reflection in the mirror.

People became blank faces and my memories from those times are a blur. Near the end of high school, I reached a point where I either had to give up or get help. Too exhausted to continue, I finally realized that life did not have to be such a struggle.

I collapsed one day in drama class, my body too exhausted to continue with the strict regime I had it on. I tried to laugh it off but ended up running down the hall to the counsellor's office in tears. I cannot remember the conversation I had with her or what I said, but I left with a phone number in my hand to call for help. And I did.

Although there have been too many ups and downs to count, I would not have it any other way. Today my objective is to bring about awareness of eating disorders without focusing on what I ate or how much I weighed.

The extreme emotions I have always run away from, I now treasure deeply. I create art not controlled by my body. This is only the beginning and I hope to touch many people along the way.

Lori Henry is a writer and actor based in Vancouver, Canada. She struggled with bulimia for six years and is now fully recovered. Her book, *Silent Screams* (978-1-4357-1843-2), is a collection of poems written during that time. She was also the publisher and editor of *Beauty: You Define It* magazine.
For more information about Lori, visit www.lorihenry.ca

Tell Me Something

Tell me that I am worth it.
Good enough to love.
Tell me not to worry.
I am fine the way I am,
Tell me that you love me
Through your honest eyes.
Just please tell me something
to disprove these murderous lies.

This Body

I am sorry for all the pain I have caused,
for all those knives I have stabbed you with.

I am sorry for all the times I have beaten you up,
for every time I have bruised you and made you sick.

I am sorry for hating you without reason,
for hiding you,
for flaunting you,
for making you feel worthless.

I am trying so hard to treat you well,
but I just cannot seem to get it right.

Yet you stand by me everyday,
giving me life and supporting me,
never judging me,
and even after all the wounds I have inflicted
you are still always there for me.
Please forgive me.

Poems by Lisa Paige

Recovery is an unbelievable number of triumphs varying in proportion. I wrote this poem after being laxative-free for a month. I remember feeling like I had accomplished something so amazing, yet the world around me never stopped to notice.

My Journey

I made it to another crest
Against disbelieving eyes
I stand exhausted, looking back,
And I said my last goodbyes

I take a moment to reflect
Upon this recent crawl
This path was full of weeds and thorns
But I beat them down one and all

So where is the big celebration?
The commemoration, the jubilee?
Why don't I feel elated?
Like I have conquered a big enemy?

It is with mixed feelings I look back
On my journey so painful and long
There are comfortable holes calling me back
Still I know going back would be wrong

They entice you with safety and freedom
Offer a sanctuary from the world outside
But the holes are so deep and the walls so steep
I am familiar with this deceptive landslide

So as I sit on this hillside and look out
At the endless peaks and valleys ahead
I am frozen with fear… which direction to go?
For I am alone on this mountain I dread

I am cold, staring at the icy summit
Unwelcoming snow covered caps
I am not sure who I am right now
So exhausted I want to collapse

I try to rest here but soon wake up
From the cries I hear deep in my sleep
For the echoes in my mind mean I must drudge on
However thorny, or slushy or steep

As I make my ascent I realize
The old voices are starting to dim
Though I am beaten and torn I am still standing
And I can feel the bright sun on my skin

I am beginning to observe a new voice
And decide to let it become known
For it has been silent for so many years
And this poor voice has been my own

The snow will be melted when I reach the peak
I believe I will make it someday
I will look out beyond at the scenery
Smile, spread my wings, and fly away

Meryl is my therapist and friend, and was the first person in my life to see the "real" me. She knows the most horrific details of my soul and loves me any way. For that I will always be grateful.

Thank You Meryl

A grown woman with a child's heart timidly walks into the room
It is cold and bright and I look at you, you are summing me up, I assume.
Your face looks nice enough; your voice is warm and kind
But I do not trust very easily, people try to get into my mind.
I cannot explain the things I do; they do not make sense to me:
The thoughts, the acts, the voices. You will definitely think I am crazy.
But after our very first meeting, you looked me in the eye
And said, "I will never leave you," hmmm… I will give you one more try.
And then one day you shared with me that I was not all alone
And that you have been down this path before,
and my feelings were well known.
I felt a special bond with you when you shared with me that day
I know you do not always do that with every client that way.
So I decided that I finally could trust you completely with my heart
And that is when I opened up and told you who tore it all apart.
When I decided to go down that path you were with me all the way
But it took quite a toll on me and I started to fade away.
But once again you took control, my best interest in your heart
And put me in the safest place, trying to give me a fresh start.
You knew how very scared I was, and you called me every day
How big a heart you have my friend, words could never say.
It takes an amazing person to break down this iron wall
And it is only with you that I am safe when the memories recall.
But no matter how much I lean on you, you remind me all the time
Of my continued success in daily life,
and the mountains that I have climbed.
I know I am taking baby steps, but making progress all the same
And soon I know I will help another girl take away the anger
and the shame.
But I will never forget the love you shared, the time, the care, the concern,
And I cannot wait until the day when I can give it back in return.

The Knock

I hear a knock upon my door
But I must have been mistaken
For there is none so brave to come up the walk
Of a house that has been forsaken

The house looks well-kept and appealing to some
But the windows and doors remain closed
If anyone dare take a peek inside
The decay of my soul is exposed

For behind these walls is a different view
Each room with a story to tell
If you dare to come in get ready to run
Before you get sucked into my lifetime of hell

This room I call my Eating Disorder
Funhouse mirrors show gigantic proportions
Swollen cheeks, calories and laxatives
Binging and purging and distortions.

That may all sound a bit crazy to you
But that was my favorite retreat
If you dare to go on I will show you more
If you promise to be discreet

This room I call SI for short
Knives and blades all around
This may be difficult to understand
But the sight of my blood calms me down

If you want to leave now I understand
For the next room is worse than the last
You see it is full of the skeletons
I have carefully hid from my past

Please be careful where you walk
As we kick up the dust and decay
Of rotten memories, of violence and abuse

I have been trying to numb all away

This next room is dark and I am so ashamed
To let anyone step inside
It is usually locked and there is only a few
With whom I choose to confide

When I let someone in, they usually run
For there is screaming and horrible cries
This is the place where I lost myself
Where the innocence of my childhood died

It gets a little messy now, here in my house
So be real careful where you step
There are a lot of open holes on the ground
And some I have recently closed up

These are from the most recent years
When I battled and fought and raged
Over several truths that came charging at me
When I saw my own children that age

Now if you are still with me and willing
I have got something else to share
It is the room where I spend the most time
Call it Loneliness, Emptiness, Despair

It is there where I allow myself anger
Let my true feelings really come through
It is also where I do lots of crying
Which is something I always feared to do

If you are still with me on this tour
Of my house that needs much assembly
Please do not step on the blades of new grass
That spring up when I let myself be Me

These blades of grass are from today, I think,
For I held a young child while he cried
And those over there are from last week

When my own hunger was not denied

As we walk through my house you start to see
There are many more rooms to explore
Some are bright and cheerful and pretty
But are you still here to knock on the door?

I know that looks are deceiving
And I am just another house on the block
But if you explore, I promise there is more
If you are only willing to knock

Lisa Paige is forty-three years old and lives in Massachusetts. She is in recovery for eating disorders suffered since early childhood. Lisa is currently working on her first poetry book. If you would like to get in touch with Lisa, you can send an email to lisapn@comcast.net

Calling in the Self
A Homecoming

By Lori B

Prologue

Someone asks me: What foods do you love?
And I answer: This is still a loaded question.

Food I have worshipped, bargained about, and wrestled with.
Food I have stolen, prayed over, fantasized about and dreamt of.
I have lied about food, hidden food, numbed myself with food
and been terrorized by it. It's hard to call this love.

It has been said that all sickness is homesickness.
And there are a million ways to leave home, everyone does it –
physically, emotionally, spiritually. People leave willingly, as a
kind of evolution, liberation and independence, or they leave
as an act of rebellion and dissolution.

The real trick is coming home.

Leaving

When I was nine years old, I started to remember my dreams which were all about traveling. For a while, I had the terrifying thought that my mind was trying to escape from my body – it was going amazing places at night without my body. But within a few years, I realized it was me who wanted to leave home.

My parents were loving, well-educated professionals (my mother was a doctor and my father was an academic and lawyer) and they were truly perplexed about my desire to leave. Feeling increasingly claustrophobic and suffocated, I was equally perplexed. My mother had shelves of promotional pills in her office from which I would select some bottles randomly, and then swallow a handful of whatever I had chosen. A counselor told me I should look up the drugs in my mother's reference guide before I took them, but I rejected her advice; if I wanted to be safe, I wouldn't be popping random pills. Russian roulette has suspense AND a bullet.

My high school experience in the late 1960s was a hippie boarding school on three-hundred acres of Vermont farmland. During those years I was never particularly thin or particularly fat and I was not overly worried about the size of my body. I had this very engaged and vivacious side but at the same time I had considerable cynicism and a lot of hidden darkness. I began to use alcohol and drugs compulsively, and this is likely why it took longer for me to find my sad groove with food – my compulsions were otherwise occupied. When I turned eighteen I remember being surprised that I had not died yet. *Pretty good,* I thought, *you survived your eighteenth birthday...*

At twenty, reeling from a romantic rejection, I tried my first real diet. A woman down the street introduced me to a low carbohydrates program and from the very beginning the sense of control was intoxicating. The world became extremely simple when I was on a food plan – Eat this, don't eat that. The bathroom scale was my arbiter of success and failure and a good day meant having been "perfect" with the food. My mother, the physician, prescribed diet pills, but I used them mainly recreationally. From then on I dabbled in diets, an amateur learning the ropes, before I hit the big time.

Some years later, during a short trip to London, I ate more chocolate than I had previously consumed in my entire lifetime. I needed a bigger pair of pants to fly home in than the ones in which I had arrived. This was a first. I was baffled by my size change and a little scared, but I chalked it up to a family crisis that had consumed me prior to the trip and to poor sexual and social boundaries with my British host. *Probably nothing a little dieting can't repair,* I thought.

Soon after my return to the United States, I moved to Los Angeles to find work in the film industry. Seemingly overnight, food threw itself into reverse and backed into me like a Mack truck. I barely knew what hit me. Food became my enemy, my master, and my nemesis. And once that beast inside me roared, it demanded feeding at all hours. Suddenly I was stalking the face of the planet, searching for more of everything – yet nothing, no amount of anything I shoveled into my body, was enough. I hunted for muffins in the morning, the bigger the better. Lunches went on for hours, spilling into dinner, until my eating became a roiling mass of undifferentiated consumption.

The trajectory of my decline was swift and steep, Superman style, "faster than a speeding bullet, more powerful than a locomotive." After several months of non-stop eating, I landed face down on the mat. The referee counted me out, the bell rang – DING! The contest was over.

I had lost to a monster that no one ever saw – a silent, invisible, punishing stalker, who knew my every move because it had taken up residence inside me. Spewing vicious epithets about my body size and shape, about my intelligence and my value, its withering assault reduced my self-esteem to rubble. The self-hatred inside this tunnel is unfathomable. This is the nightmare many women call their lives.

I stuck my finger down my throat once but could not vomit – a failure for which I am now deeply grateful, but about which, on that day, I cursed myself. I prayed for a 'designer disease,' something with a name people could respect – Anorexia, Bulimia – but instead I shambled through my days bingeing like an abandoned dog living on the street. I masqueraded as functional, getting dressed in the morning, going to work, and paying my rent, but I became increasingly disorganized and ashamed over my secret life with food.

Eventually, I brushed the crumbs off the front of my shirt and crawled into an Overeaters Anonymous meeting. Sadly, the abstinence I found at that time was very rigid and not much different than a diet. What I needed desperately was to cultivate some self-love and flexibility, but instead I careened between fear (on my bad days) and arrogance (on my good ones). When I had a slip and ate something off my food plan, there was no bounce – my abstinence shattered into a thousand pieces and I was off and running again.

One day, I got caught in a terrible food storm, a car binge that took me from store to restaurant to store through the afternoon and into the evening. This is the drill – something like a combination of duck, duck, goose and musical chairs, I had to find a way to end the night at home with one last portion. But the beast always tricked me into devouring everything immediately, so I had to stop again, buy more food, and when it was gone, stop again, buy more food – it is a very tough game to win. Somehow I made it home. I slammed the door, grabbed a spoon, and rushed with my package to the rocking chair on the balcony. Eating and crying, my stomach full beyond bursting, it dawned on me that I was killing myself. I saw a cartoon of the spoon as a weapon, slipping in and out of my throat, stuffing me, gagging me.

I must not want to be here.

I must not want to **be** at all.

Then all the food was gone and I was weeping into the empty take-out container. Suddenly, I understood why people check out, why people take their own lives. I called my sister and she made me call a suicide hotline. The next day, I began making preparations to return to New York.

Coming Back

I wish I could say that my recovery has been as rapid or as linear as my descent into the inferno. I wish I could say my recovery has been perfect or is complete. As they say, it got worse before it got better. In between the bingeing I began to fast for a day or two as a way to reassert a sense of control. This evolved into longer and longer fasts. Dangerously haywire, I lived in this flip-flopped netherworld of extremes – Binge, starve, binge, starve, my two-step rollercoaster through hell. I love this definition of addiction – doing the same thing over and over and expecting different results.

I went back to twelve-step meetings and twice-weekly psychotherapy in New York. These two crucial supports kept me from going further over the brink into madness or self-annihilation. Lumbering around the city in baggy black clothing, feeling invisible, I socialized with street people and went in and out of my mania with food.

I read a lot of books in my search for wellness. One, Susie Orbach's groundbreaking *Fat is a Feminist Issue*, told me the trouble was some blistering seed of self-hatred that had lodged inside me and taken root. This had something to do with why I felt possessed, why I felt that it was me, but somehow also not me, who made these painful choices with food and punctuated my thoughts with venomous self-criticism.

When I got my first glimmer that being WHOLE is what I am after – not being perfect – it began to dawn on me that my recovery was likely to be incremental rather than abrupt. I still prayed that I might find a miracle cure, but I began to sense that getting well would be a long road of ups and downs, more about recovering a self than about a particular way to eat.

Reading *Overcoming Overeating* by Jane Hirschmann and Carol Munter I gained some practical tools for ending the binge-starve cycle. I began to recognize that the fasting, in fact, *fed* the bingeing, and I began to believe that ending deprivation was key to stabilizing my relationship with food. Hirschmann and Munter recommended two incredible practices that were terrifying but wildly liberating.

First, they encouraged filling my pantry or frig with the foods that most triggered me so that it would be impossible for me to eat it all in one sitting. This messes with the first law of bingeing – you must eat until everything is gone. Second, they suggested something called "demand feeding" – carrying food with me at all times and feeding myself the moment I felt hungry. This is what it must be like to breast-feed a baby, very tender and responsive and loving. From the time my eating had gone completely out of whack, it was my head that dictated when, what, and how much food to consume. My stomach just happened to be the receptacle where it all landed. Demand feeding required serious re-training, cultivating the ability to acknowledge when I was hungry and then the willingness to really feed myself rather than ignore the signals or stuff something down my gullet to shut me up. This practice was a quantum shift towards health.

I remember, in my mid 30's, married, reasonably happy, and much more stable, I stopped at a grocery store on the way home after a sushi dinner and a wonderful, loving evening with my sister. Back in the car, unconsciously, reflexively, I pulled a few grapes from the bag and began to put them in my mouth.

No, I thought, Wait. I just had a beautiful time with Lisey. If I eat these grapes I might chase away that feeling. Am I willing to let this love fill me and be enough?

For the first time, I articulated that I had an ABSORPTION problem – a problem recognizing my feelings, in general, and a problem receiving satisfaction from good feelings in particular. This was fascinating! So I sat in the car and I used my own hands to pat my body lightly – my arms, my belly, up and down my legs, my face – and in this way I literally "pushed" the goodness into my skin and encouraged myself to digest my own experience. I have repeated this technique many times since then because the pace of the world sometimes leaves me feeling like I am traveling in a rocket ship and I need to slow down to absorb this life of mine.

Homecoming

Bringing my body home to the east was only the very beginning of bringing my Self home to my body. I always suspected that parts of me were missing, had been sent away somewhere for safekeeping so I began exploring "calling in the self" as a practice. With care and compassion, I invite all those pieces of me that had flown away, splintered, during times of hopeless darkness to come home and live with me again. I let them know that I can brook their sadness. I can fold them into the fullness of who I am today.

I have to admit, I still leave every once in a while, check-out, but I have faith that I will return. And when I do, I welcome myself home.

Lori B lives in San Francisco and is a survivor of eating disorders. After a stint in the film business, she trained and practiced as a body-centered psychotherapist in New York City. She has performed and taught various kinds of healing, dancing, music, and ritual in theaters and living rooms around the world. For more information about her music, photography, writing, and private coaching work, please visit www.loriB.net

Lori B's song, *bodyMine* is featured on the *You Are Not Alone Companion CD.*

Poems by Mackenzie Brooks

Road Trip

A trip to a magical and mysterious destination,
Sometimes we get lost, completely turned around,
Roads seem to never end.
And some days the storms come and through the rain
We cannot see the road signs, our directions to our amazing destination.
We start to lose hope thinking we will never get to where we want to go
But when we are just about to give up,
About to turn around and head back to where we started,
The sun comes peeking through the rain clouds, helping us to see the road signs once again,
Revealing to us where we are on our journey.
Then after time we start to run low on gas, no gas station for miles.
We keep pushing forward, driving on fumes, feeling like we will run out of gas at any moment.
Then when we think the car will go no further we find a gas station, just in the nick of time.
After we fill up, we feel like we could drive on forever, never having any problems!
But eventually you run low again.
And sometimes you are not going to get to the gas station in time, you will have to push.
Step out of your comfort zone and work a little to get where you need to go.
Then, even though you had to push, you eventually get to another gas station and everything is fine again.
When all you want to do is drive straight through to our final destination, it is discouraging when you have to make pit stops.
But no matter how many times you have to make these stops, the things holding you back from where you want to be,
You have to have faith you will get there.
There will be many unpaved roads.
Bumps.
Potholes.
But these are just roads, you will get to the smooth ones again,

Making your journey seem so easy.
Do not try to take short cuts,
Follow your directions, or you may miss something amazing.
There may be nails in the road,
You do not see it but you lose control,
And see the damage it has done to your tire.
Just one more set back. Do not get discouraged.
You have got a spare.
More hope.
Fix your situation, change your tire, take a deep breath, get back behind the wheel, drive!
Strap yourself in and enjoy the ride!
When you reach your destination you realize all the rough mileage was more than worth it!

True Beauty

We all notice beauty from the moment we open our eyes in the mornings.
The beauty in the sunshine,
The beauty of the birds singing their beautiful songs.
Beauty of the flowers standing so boldly.
Beauty in the sky stretched out up above.
But the truth is,
Until you can see beauty in the reflection in the mirror,
And know there is beauty inside of that woman staring back at you,
You do not actually see the true beauty in anything else.
These things you thought were so beautiful before are so much more vibrant.
More exciting.
More beautiful.
When you realize God made everything from the beautiful sunrise in the morning,
To the beautiful sunset in the evening,
And everything in between,
How could you not see the beauty in the reflection?
God does not make mistakes.
The stormy days,
Gray and dark,
Are not a mistake.
And these days have their own beauty.
When a flower has not bloomed yet,
Still shut up tightly in its bud,
It is <u>not</u> a mistake,
And it is beautiful.
And the women staring back at you,
Longing to feel beautiful,
Longing for you to love her as she is,
Is not a mistake.
And she is beautiful.
Inside,
And out!

Mackenzie Brooks, a seventeen-year-old student from Texas, is in recovery from anorexia.

Blemish, Balance, Beauty

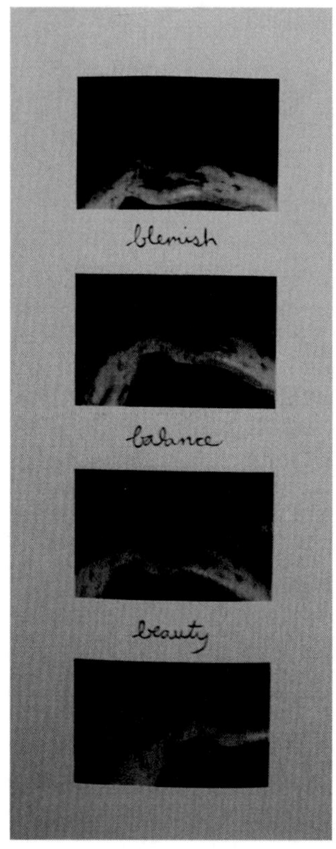

"I created this piece as I was wrestling with issues of how to find beauty within myself and my body, while accepting my 'blemishes.' The images are semi-distorted, inked-over photographs, portraying the human body with blemished skin balancing in difficult positions. I was exploring the concept of how to find a point of balance between blemish and beauty to reach wholesomeness."

On Facing The Lens

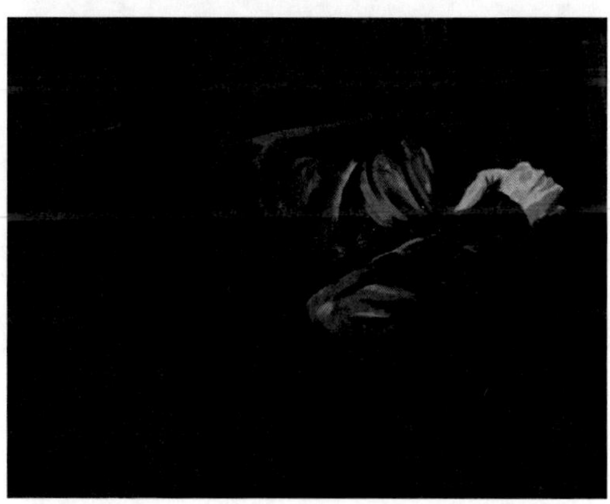

"These paintings depict a girl cowering in front of a 'lens.' I got the idea to do these paintings when I was photographing a friend who was abrasive to being photographed, and her physical response to the camera was very much like this. She cowered away from it and was afraid to be 'exposed.' That metaphor can be used in a much wider scope... not only when facing a camera, but also when having to face ourselves, to look honestly at our problems, to face our fears, to face the world with our flaws."

A Lament

"This piece addresses sexual abuse, which has been an underlying aggravator of my eating disorder. The photo is a self-portrait toned with tea stain and oil paint. After the staining, I cracked the emulsion of the photo surface. I am addressing the silent pain that sits inside survivors of sexual abuse, which I think is a necessary thing to face in order to regain self and confidence."

Holly Elzinga, a twenty-six-year old artist from Chicago, Illinois, struggled with bulimia and finds strong healing power in creating art.

Poems by Lucie Beardwood

No matter how many times you get knocked down – no matter how dark you feel it is, there is always a little light glowing in your heart!

My Little Light

A little light of hope
is glowing in my heart
I feel it through the depths of my soul

had been blown out but still lay smouldering
waiting for a spark

I will cup my hands around it to keep it safe from harm
give it fuel to help it grow strong
nurture it until it shines so brightly
showing the world the true me
setting me free.

My mum is my angel; I am so lucky to have her fighting at my side.

My Angel

I have a battle to fight
But
An angel stands beside me so I know I will be alright
She
Gives me strength to fight each demon
The war inside my mind
She is ever with me
Sharing her compassion and patience
Sharing her courage and wisdom

I have a battle to fight
But
An angel stands beside me so I know I will be alright

© Lucie Beardwood

This poem says a lot about my feelings while I was ill, about the feeling that I was a stranger to myself, that I did not know who I was or who I was supposed to be, about the tiredness and the feelings of hopelessness that the illness brings.

I Pray

I pray for the courage to stay alive through this hell
I pray for the strength to fight this battle
I pray for the tools to rid myself of the poison in my soul
I pray for the energy to use them and the wisdom to try
I pray for the struggle in my mind to finally end
I pray for the will to keep my faith through all adversity
I pray for the power to stay true to myself
I pray for the insight to know myself when I become it
I pray for the ability to keep my dreams alive
I pray for the memory to recall my family's love and support in my darkest hours
I pray for your love, support, compassion, patience
And everlasting love

I decided to think of all the things I would like to do and all of the things I would be able to do if I kept fighting and got better. There is still a lot on the list that I have not got around to yet, but I'm working on it.

I Dream

I dream……
I dream of being well
I dream of gaining peace of mind
I dream of enjoying family times
I dream of being able to forgive and forget
I dream of travelling the world and visiting Tibet
I dream of dreaming
I dream of gaining wisdom from all situations
I dream of writing and publishing a book
I dream of being able to heal myself
I dream of being able to heal others
I dream of endless energy
I dream of getting a puppy
I dream of treating myself without feeling guilty
I dream of getting a degree
I dream of being able to see life's colours again
I dream of being myself
I dream of being happy with who I am
I dream of living
I dream……

Writing this helped me when I thought I had no innocence left. It helped me to see that there are many aspects of me and many different parts to my character. Imagining my inner child helped me to want to look after myself and be patient and kind to myself.

Precious Inner Child

'Hello' I smile at myself
My inner child
The little me
Something is wrong here
I see fear in her eyes
She sits shivering and frail
Vulnerable and alone
'What are you afraid of?' I ask
She stares at me
Her eyes filling with tears
'You' she answers
I look at her huddled in the corner, in the dark
She is cold, afraid, abandoned
By me
I want to cuddle her
And tell her that it will all be okay.
I want to say 'I am sorry'
I ask what I can do for her
'I am hungry' she replies
I can see a yearning, a desperate need for
Food
I can see that she is tired
Of battling with me
Tired of my punishment
Tired of live without my love.

I walk forwards, arms held ready to
Embrace her
A fragile smile appears on her dry
Lips
'I promise to never neglect you or
Hurt you again' I say
I will help you to get through this, I will

Help you to survive
My precious inner child.

Lucie Beardwood, from Wales (and proud of it!), is a student at the London School of Journalism and is working on her first novel. She currently lives in Gloucestershire, with her two adorable dogs – Deeva the Lhasa Apso and Toby the terror (sorry, Terrier). Lucie struggled with body image issues and disordered eating for many years, culminating in hospitalization and treatment for anorexia. Now that she is recovered, it is her passion to support others in their recovery. She is part of an inspirational eating disorder recovery channel on YouTube.
(www.youtube.com/user/lifeembracing).
If you want to get in touch with Lucie, feel free to send her an email at lucie@youarenotalonebook.com

Poems by Cat S.Ginn

I wrote this poem when I realized how many times I left a tiny bit of myself behind me as I lived my life – a bit of my heart here, my soul there... my memory here, my love there... when one of my friends had died, I would lose a part of me... when I would help someone on the forums that had threatened suicide, and I had helped them... part of me was lost, though in a good way... when I create a work of art part of me goes with it... when I write a poem, part of me is left behind each time it is read.

Just This Side Of Normal

Just this side of normal
is where I sit
Just this side of normal
on top of all this

Just waiting and waiting
for something to ease
to make me feel better
for life to appease

But alas, nothing happens
no salve to my soul
Nothing to help me
begin to be whole

So onward and upward
and forward I go
just plodding along
in step with this road

This road that I've chosen
(or has been "chosen" for me)
grows narrower and steeper
and harder to see

And among all the pebbles

strewn cross my way
are pieces of myself
with nothing to say

I don't know whether
to stop and pick up
these pieces of me
that I've now seen close up

They're crying and bleeding
They're dying inside
They're wanting somehow
to wash out with the tide

But to do so, I'd lose them
A part of my soul
And then, well then...
I'd never be whole

So softly, and tenderly
I scoop them to me
And brush them off
and I save them tenderly

For these pieces are part
of my aura, my life,
an integral part
of each sorrow and strife

But mostly, I think,
as I stoop by the shore,
washing off the pieces
that I so adore....

Mostly, they're part
of my every pain
and I'd have to choose
whether to do it again

And I guess if I had to
I'd have to say yes

Because I am who I am
because of all THIS,

For we are what we have learned,
don't you think?
We ARE what we eat
We ARE what we drink

And turning away
from all that we've been
won't keep us from being
the same way again.

It just will only prolong
the inevitable things
Like how your heart soars
and how your soul sings

But time can't erase
that you ARE who you ARE
And you cannot run from that
no matter how far...

...you go in the distance
to leave where you've been
you take some parts with you
to do over again.

So maybe, just maybe
time doesn't heal
It just makes us a newer,
more different deal

And we learn to accept it
eventually, so you see....
Eventually we accept
That You are You, and this is me.

The Recovery

I woke up this morning and didn't even care
That the scale sat in the closet over there
I put on my jeans and didn't even know
That the button on them buttoned just so…
I looked in the mirror, and didn't even see
A horrible person, staring back at me
And what to my wondering eyes should appear
But a reflection staring back, with love, not despair
But I didn't stop to think about things like that
I just grabbed my coat, and my boots and my hat
For today was the first day, I can even remember
That life held pure passion, and even a glimmer
Of things that were good, of things giving hope
And the voice of ED… did I hear him? Nope.
Did I even notice that he had gone away?
Did I even take notice he wasn't here today?
And now that I think back to the rest of the week
Wow… he's been missing, I haven't heard a peep...
Just when did this happen, I wondered aloud
When had my head been void of the crowd
Of voices that always were saying to me
"You're fat! You're worthless," when? Could it be…
That I had recovered, and didn't even know it?
But my body? And my soul… and my mind did they show it?
So I looked at myself in the mirror real well
And I looked for some signs of recovery, but hell,
I didn't know what recovery looked like, not really
And standing there staring, I kinda felt silly
But I stood there and stared, and then stared some more
Before I turned and walked out the door…
What now was missing? What would I do?
Ed was gone, Were we through?
Was he gone completely, just out of my life?
I should be so ecstatic… No strife.
For THIS was what I had waited for so long
To be able to breathe, and sing freedom's song
And I finally realized the emptiness I was feeling
Way down in the pit of my stomach, I was reeling

For I hadn't known this feeling in forever, even younger…
I nearly cried as I realized..… it was HUNGER!
And as tears rained down my face, I was surprised
They were tears of happiness raining from my eyes!
Was it over, maybe not, but I knew in my heart
That at least… at the Very least, it was a damn good start!

HORizonTaL LieS

I have pulled down the shades,
And I've locked all the doors
I've taken down the signs
HE don't live here anymore
But still he came knocking
And still he did call
And still I hear footsteps
Echo in the hall
I swear I didn't call him
At all here today
I swear I didn't whisper
His name when I prayed
I swear to you now
As I fall on my knees
Oh won't you believe in me

Please?

For I've carried him around
On my waist and my hips
And my butt has been bad-mouthed
By his two lying lips
And he's sat there and told me
Through year after year
Come closer dear, weak one
I'm here…

And he leers…

But now I say to you
I swear to you now
I didn't, I didn't
Invite that mad cow!
He came uninvited
Just walked in the door
And I found him there lying
Dead on the floor

I've poked him, And I've prodded
And called him some names
I've offered him milk
And to play some lame games
But he lies there so still
And a breath? None he takes
He's either dead…
Or a corpse he now fakes
So if you won't be minding,
Can you drag him outside?
I've met him a few times,
And usually he lied…
Some boasting and pretending
To be my good friend
But here's where that friendship
Shall end.

There's no love lost between us,
I won't mourn or cry
He'd usually leave me
With a Horizontal Lie
Would turn me to a mirror
Or put me on a scale
I called it
My own living hell

So, go on. And take him
Just drag him away
Poor ED… **deaD ED**
I hope you STAY that way!

Cat S. Ginn is forty-seven-years-old and has struggled with an eating disorder for most of her life, but was not diagnosed as anorexic until around her fortieth birthday.

Cat, who is also bipolar and a survivor of childhood sexual abuse, has been married for over twenty-five years to a wonderful man, and she is a loving mother to two children, aged twenty and fifteen. Cat, who has a BS in Art and Marketing, has written poetry and created art pieces since the age of four. Her lifelong dream is to publish her own poetry book and to sell her art. She has the love and support of her family and her best friend, Mutt.

She is currently in therapy with a wonderful therapist on a weekly basis and has been at normal weight for about five years... and though she still hears Ed's voice (the eating disorder voice) inside her head, she considers herself in recovery and winning.

Tree Goddess

"My inspiration was that I started feeling more in-tune with the earth around me, and felt rooted to the earth, my surroundings, and more like the world was one with me. My family, my friends, my children were all parts of me, because before that it felt no one understood me or cared… It was a revelation of sorts, to feel that finally, the world cared, and understood what was happening to me, and was helping me to be grounded again."

Give It A Rest Dali

"This is a spin on my favorite artist, Salvadore Dali, who inspires me with his surreal paintings and drawings. This jumble of a work came at me during a pretty hard time while I was in the psych ward for cutting myself during a manic state (cutting is a self-inflicted, self-soothing, self-controlled method of soothing oneself that I would come to understand was covering up inside pain with an outside pain, much as anorexia was doing). Besides having anorexia, I also suffer from Bipolar Disorder (Type I), rapid cycling. During this week in the hospital, I created about six different pieces of art (which happens a lot during my manic phases). This particular piece in a rush of mania, with no real focus, except that I remember thinking things like: 'Head over heels,' 'Fish out of water,' 'Foot in mouth,' 'Hand me that.' I was a jumbled mess, and was reeling from mania/anorexia/cutting... but finally with medication and help from others I was able to help quiet my mind. Art is healing for me, it is beautiful, it is soothing, and it calms my spirit. This piece is one of my favorites because it helped so much to get OUT what was hurting inside."

One Eyed Peggy

"My inspiration for her came from down deep… See? She is crying... she started from there... I started at her eye... and drew her slimness with nowhere to go except to the hand who could help her... but it was not for clothing that she searched, not to cover herself... she was not ashamed... she was looking to find a way to TELL someone what was wrong... It APPEARS that she is paying for the boot, the foot (or even another peg leg) that she needs, when really, if you look closely at the drawing, you will see that she is actually trying to find her voice... look at the top of the boot she is paying for... there is a set of lips laying there silently... it is her VOICE. She has found her voice. You see, people with anorexia, bulimia, EDNOS, and other eating disorders often do not have 'voices,' or do not use them... she is crying because she has been so long without her voice... she does not know HOW to articulate what it is that she needs... and now, she has finally found someone who has SO much that she needs, she does not know what to get first... she has finally found her voice... the question is... will she be able to speak? Will she be able to SAY what she needs to say? And will anyone listen?"

Sight

By Jessica

I can never repay what you gave to me
You gave me the **eyes**
Which helped me to **see**
Eyes to see
The person inside
And the strength for me
Not to *run* and *hide*
I **learned** about who I was
And the feelings I had
I learned that my feelings
Were not wrong **or** bad
I began to **understand** the person in the mirror
You helped me to see myself a lot clearer
For this I am **grateful**
And can never repay
I want you to know
I am living each day
I continue to **blossom**
With a soul that *shines* bright
And none of this I'd have now
Had you not given me my *sight*

Jessica, a twenty-eight-year-old student and writer from Houston, Texas, is recovered from anorexia, bulimia, COE (Compulsive Overeating), self-injury, drug and alcohol abuse, and contributed her recovery story to *You Are Not Alone, Volume I.* Jessica is an eating disorder awareness and prevention actionist and women's issues actionist. For more information, and to get in touch with Jessica, visit www.live-out-loud.org

My Story

By Angela Minard

Who is Claudia? She is not my friend, but she has been a part of my life for a very long time. I am forty years old and she has been hanging around since I was seven. She is the voice of my anorexia, and she has almost taken my life numerous times.

I have an amazing therapist and nutritionist who thought it would be a good idea to give my eating disorder a separate identity from myself. It would be a way to delineate between my own voice and the voice of the eating disorder. I am finally beginning to see how often Claudia talks to me. She is bossy, demanding, snide, snotty, and degrading. She also reinforces what she says when I do it.

I want to try to fight back. Will I be able to argue and disagree when she tells me how fat and disgusting I am? "You don't need to eat," she will say.

I remember the first time she spoke to me. I was seven years old, sitting in church, and looking down at my thighs as I sat in the pew. "Your legs are so fat!" she said.

Why did she choose that moment to begin her torment? I am not really sure. My mom, grandma, and two aunts were constantly dieting and discussing their weight. I am sure that their conversations wormed their way into what I began to also believe about myself. Being raped at the age of eleven was the real beginning of my self-loathing and hatred. Puberty began soon after, and with it, the ultimate betrayal of my own body.

It took some time for Claudia to tell me her name. She knows that it may very well destroy her, but she does not get to make all of the decisions anymore! Sometimes I am not even sure that I want to destroy her. She is the one with the control most of the time, but I know that needs to change if I am to survive. I am married to a wonderful and supportive husband, and we have four beautiful sons. I have so much to live for, and Claudia cannot have my life anymore!

Angela Minard, who is married with four sons, is forty-years-old and lives in the United States. She has struggled with an eating disorder for many years, and is now in recovery. She is also a childhood rape survivor. If you want to get in touch with Angela, you can send an e-mail to angminard@kc.surewest.net or visit her website at www.poetrypoem.com/4angel

"Secrets" was one of the first poems I wrote when I began my therapy. I had kept my rape a secret for over thirty years before I shared it first with my husband, and then my therapist, and finally my mother. It was my way of saying, "I trust you with all that I am." The beginning of my letting go.

Secrets

I am afraid all of the time. I wonder what you hide.
No one is who they really are.
Who are you? Who am I?
Who can I trust with all that I am?
For so long you have seen what I want you to see, or so I thought.
I do not want to be alone anymore.
To be me.
Alive.
So I give all of my secrets away,
To hold like a wish in your hands.
A deep breath...
And then gone...

© Angela Minard

I wrote 'Echo' soon after I wrote 'Secrets.' I was beginning to feel a sense of hope and freedom. I could finally hear the laughter again. It was a wonderful feeling!

Echo

Echo Echo hear the sound of silence all around.
Screaming quiet underneath the depth of water blue.
Hear me! Wash away this pain.
Let the tears fall down like rain.
Dive down deep and cleanse my soul.
Find my voice. Make me whole.
Echo Echo hear the sound of laughter all around.

© Angela Minard

My Worries

"My first counselor asked me to write down the things that worried me the most. I do not worry about my weight these days, but if I ever find myself counting my imperfections or feeling insecure about my weight then I know that something is going on inside me and that I have to check in with my emotions and get to the root of what was bothering me."

Love

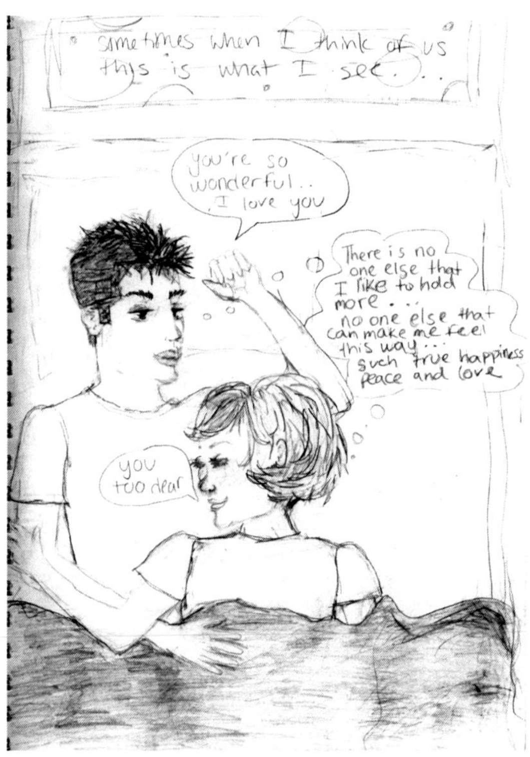

"This is me and my boyfriend. He and I met just before I went into my treatment and he has helped me so much. We have been together for three years."

Linder Dwyer is twenty-three years old and lives in Texas. She struggled with anorexia for one year and with bulimia for four. Now that Linder is recovered, she is experiencing life fully and pursuing her dream of becoming a counselor, and having a good relationship.
"I am proof that you can actually get past it!"

Joy's Recovery Story

By Joy Nollenberg

I had had eating issues in one form or another for about thirteen years, from the age of ten till I was twenty-three. I pretty much fit every stereotype of the "typical" anorexic – I was a high achiever in school; I was a people-pleaser; my dad barely spoke; my mom was the personification of Dr. Jekyll / Mr. Hyde; and so on. I also covered a few of the stereotypical 'thin' sports: I started ballet when I was four years old and did that until I was twelve, at which point I started figure skating, then cheerleading in high school and college. I never really purged. I tried, but I just could never really make it work. I used to get so frustrated, but in hindsight, I am so grateful I never learned to do that.

Fast forward to the year I ended up recovering.

Why did I recover? When did I recover? And why was I successful?

Because I literally had no choice.

I had finished my last semester at college (fall semester), but was still on the cheer team (spring semester), and I was being forced to meet with the team doctors every week in order to be cleared for practice. I was finally benched after a few not-so-good EKGs, blood pressure measurements, and so on. I had been living with two friends of mine, who were also my teammates. Prior to moving in with them, I had considered them two of my best friends. Unfortunately, they did not really understand the eating disorder. At first, they tried to be 'helpful,' saying they would support me no matter what. But when their 'help' ended up being yelling at me almost every day for not eating enough, and telling me I was lazy and selfish and all that, we did not get along so well any more.

I was referred to an eating disorder treatment program at a local hospital. When I went in for my intake assessment I met with a medical doctor, a psychologist, and a dietician. I had blood drawn, a bunch of tests taken, peed in a cup, and was weighed (backwards, of course). After the staff members met to discuss what was best for me, their official recommendation was that I did either an inpatient or outpatient program as soon as possible. Evidently, my heart rate was low, my blood pressure was orthostatic, and my body temperature was low. Unfortunately, there was not an opening in inpatient, so they set me up with daily outpatient appointments until I could get into the full program. After I did the outpatient program for about two weeks, they called and left a message on my answering machine saying that my insurance company was refusing to pay, and as a result, they could not see me any more. After making a huge deal over how much I needed to be there, and how I would not survive if I did not get medical monitoring right away, they left me a message with referrals to some free walk-in counseling places in the ghetto. Nice. So they basically told me to go home and try not to die.

I honestly thought that that was it. I guess I did not think that it was possible to recover without intensive treatment. I thought I did not have any hope left. I had tried everything to get into another program – social workers had been trying to find some other treatment center for me for months, with no luck. So I literally went home and was like "This is it. I am going to die, and no one cares. No one will save me. No one will help me. I am truly on my own." I thought that was the lowest I could get.

Well, shortly thereafter, my roommates kicked me out. They gave me a week to move. However, I was very sick. I had not been working all that much, so I really could not afford to live on my own. Besides, my current rent was really cheap and Minneapolis was in a major housing shortage, so finding a new place for me to stay, that I could afford, would be challenging. Not only that, but I did not have a car and no one would help me move, so I needed to find somewhere close by. Out of desperation, I found a place a few blocks away. I knew it was not a good place before I moved in, but I did not feel like I had a choice. And I thought, "Well, nobody really wants me around anyway, so I might as well just go there and rot and wither away and disappear." And trust me, lugging your mattress down the street in the middle of January in Minnesota when you are sick and weak is not much fun at all.

I stopped working, and I no longer went to class. I literally had nowhere to be and no one to be with. I got into a pattern of sleeping all day and drinking all night. Sometimes I would exercise, usually at two a.m., after having a few drinks, until I started to worry about the calories in all that alcohol.

My life was literally going nowhere.

I had nothing to do, no plans, no anything. A whole lot of nothing.

And I remembered the days when I was systematically getting rid of any responsibilities, ties to anything, any stress that would interfere with my weight loss efforts and then I began thinking, *Is this really what I was aiming for?* This sucks!

I guess for a long time, a lot of my eating disorder was motivated by not feeling like I had 'permission to exist.' It was like a kind of test – I would slowly kill myself while everyone was watching. If they let me go, then I had my answer, and I would know I was not wanted here. I figured if they wanted me around, they would 'save' me… although ironically, when people tried to reach out and 'save' me, it made me really angry. And I guess I felt at that point in my life everyone HAD abandoned me. I WAS alone. ALL alone. Nobody even knew where I was. And then, the 'me' in me got mad – I mean really, really, really mad. I thought of all the other people in the world, who just went about their daily lives without a care in the world, doing whatever they wanted as if it were no big deal. And I thought, "Well, nobody ever bothered to ask ME if they were 'allowed' to exist. Nobody ever asked ME if they were allowed to make mistakes, to take up space, to step on my toes, or to just BE."

And then I figured, well, **if they do not need permission,** _then neither do I._

I guess you could actually say that my recovery, for me, was a big "SCREW YOU!" back at the world around me. It was like revenge, almost. I felt so unwanted, so unloved. For so long, I had lived my life trying to be everything that everyone ever wanted me to be; doing all the 'right' things, in the 'right' way, trying to make everyone like me. And then I felt like I had given myself away – I had stopped living my life, just so I could meet some arbitrary definition of 'good enough.' And I finally just said, "Screw this!" And I was hit with this sudden realization – I HAVE NOTHING TO LOSE. Literally. No matter what I did, no matter which direction I chose, anything, anywhere, anyhow was better than where I was. So I felt oddly free – *liberated*, almost. There was nowhere to go but up. Not only that, but I had systematically removed myself from the larger world of society. I had successfully absolved myself of all responsibilities, ended all friendships, ceased anything that required me to interact with anyone or anything. I had basically cleaned house on my life. I had lost a lot of good stuff, but I had also managed to cut out some really bad things, too.

And so I chose to begin rebuilding my life, brick by brick, step by step, until I was living a life that I CHOSE. No more living by other people's rules, living to impress people, to live up to some sort of arbitrary standard… life from then on would be different. It would be on MY terms.

<u>And THAT was the real turning point for me.</u>

I CHOSE to live MY life MY way.

And no one was going to stop me.

So, I moved out of that rundown house.

I started looking for a full-time job.

I started to (gasp!) EAT again. I spent the next month living with three different people in two different states. Almost every week I packed up all of my possessions and moved to a new place where I slept on the floor. I do not even remember if I ever bothered to explain why I had moved out of my place. I do not think anyone really asked.

During that time, I surfed the internet for my OWN apartment – I figured no one would kick me out if I lived alone, and I was done with trying to be close to people. I interviewed for a position as a preschool teacher and got the job. I was supposed to start on February 2nd, 2002. So, February 1st, 2002, I moved into my own downtown Minneapolis apartment – maxing out a small credit card in order to pay for the first month's rent and security deposit.

So, on February 2nd, 2002, I started my first day of work at an upper-class preschool/day care located in a high-rise in the business district of downtown Minneapolis.

Let me say this, two-year-olds NEVER sit still. And you can NEVER relax around them. They need constant supervision, especially when there are twelve of them roaming around in one room. I learned very quickly that if I hoped to survive at my job, I would need to learn to actually give my body fuel.

On my first day, I had not brought lunch with me, but I had had some breakfast. By lunchtime, I was exhausted, starving, and getting cranky. I remember being 'brave' and eating something I would not normally eat. I had horrible stomach cramps, got really dizzy… I was so frustrated that I could not just wave a magic wand and suddenly be healthy and have energy and all that. It made me really mad that my body would not just work when I needed it to.

I learned very quickly that eating 'normally' again would not be an easy task. Once I increased my intake, it was like something in me just snapped, and I was hungry every single second.

I had somehow convinced myself that increasing my intake while getting myself back in the gym (so I could burn off the calories every night) was a wonderful strategy.

Let me tell you: IT IS NOT A GOOD IDEA!

I started packing a lunch of 'safe' foods, and making an effort to eat something every day before I left for work. My biggest problem became the nighttime. After a day of constantly moving around, constantly chasing kids, then stopping at the gym for some cardio before heading home… I was HUNGRY! Looking back, I cannot even imagine how much of an energy deficit my body must have been in by the time I got home. I would go home and have dinner, which I had carefully planned. I figured I would start with 'safe' foods that fit into all the different food groups that should be included in a 'normal' dinner. And then… I would still be hungry. And I would suddenly get all excited and tell myself "It is okay! I am in recovery! I can eat food now!" And I would eat. I would start out every meal saying, "I am recovering. This is a GOOD thing I am doing. I can eat and enjoy food again now!" Ten minutes later, I would find myself in a state of extreme anxiety, mad at what I had just done, berating myself for being so stupid to think that it was okay to eat, wishing I had not done that, and wishing I had actually developed the ability to purge before.

I did try to purge, but it did not really work. So, I would tell myself I could not go to bed until I burned it all off through exercise. But something had already changed for me a bit. What, I do not know. But I would exercise for ten minutes and then suddenly my mood would change and I would stop. I would go to bed. I would feel okay.

I never really realized how sick I had become until I started getting better. I cannot remember when I started to feel cold and dizzy all the time, but I definitely noticed when it stopped. I did not notice when my energy-starved brain started tuning out background noise, but I noticed when I finally heard it again. It was not until I actually felt closer to 'fine' that I realized just how painful starvation is. The constant muscle aches, the headaches, feeling my heart pounding from dehydration, nearly passing out every time I stood up too fast, my hands so dry they would crack and bleed no matter how much lotion I used, the agonizing over whether or not I had the energy to walk across the room, the feeling that everything was too bright, too loud, too stressful, too confusing – just altogether TOO MUCH…

It was around that time that I would wake up in the middle of the night in a cold sweat, craving food like mad. I would wake up in the morning in a panic, berating myself for being so stupid to think I was allowed to eat again, wishing I had never decided to recover.

I started to dread going home. My little place of my own – a symbol of me branching out, a girl on her own in the city, my start of a new life, the place where I would reclaim who I was – my apartment started to feel different to me. I did not want to be there. That was the place where I ate. I started applying for a second job. I just wanted to be away all the time, so I would never have to go back to that kitchen where I was not in control anymore.

So I spent the next few months swinging violently back and forth between recovery and wanting to quit recovery. One minute, I would be one hundred percent into recovery. And five minutes later, I would be beating myself up for ever trying recovery. Words cannot even describe just how extreme the change would be from minute to minute.

The night bingeing was happening a bit too often, and I had been trying to cope by restricting. I somehow convinced myself that if I was going to take in enough calories for 'recovery' anyway, I might as well do that during my binge time. Well, NOT A GOOD IDEA!

My mood swings were insane – they made me feel like I was losing my mind. Sometimes when I started eating, I would get high, like literally, ecstatically HIGH. But after eating, I would flip to the other end of the spectrum. One particular night, I remember feeling such tremendous anxiety that I found myself turning all my lights off, huddling in a corner with my arms around my knees, rocking myself in an attempt to comfort myself.

I felt lost, and I did not know how to go about learning to eat normally again. I spent some time on the internet, and I found an advertisement for a research study that was taking place at my university. They did a quick interview over the phone to see if I qualified, and they said to come in for an assessment in a few months.

During this time, I was still in cheerleading. Hockey runs through March and even into May if you make it to the finals (we did, the National Championships, even!), so I was still being forced to visit the team's medical doctor (who really did not understand eating disorders at all). I happened to mention that I had signed up for this research study. Well, I do not know if he actually pulled any strings or not, but he said that he actually knew the guy in charge of it. All I know is that I got a call a week later, and they said they 'suddenly' had an opening before the end of the month.

Let us fast forward to the research study. It was a study where people were divided into groups. Some got medications; some got guided self-help, and some just got a self-help book. I got the self-help book and was supposed to go back and meet with one of the research people for fifteen minutes every few weeks at first, then every six months, and then finish up with a final assessment.

The self-help program was EXACTLY what I needed. It outlined specific steps I could take in order to re-establish normal eating habits. The first step was to start eating at scheduled times, every three or four hours, all day long, regardless of whether I binged in between or not. Trust me, it was not easy to convince myself that I really needed to eat that often. And at first, it seemed ridiculous to be continuing to eat at those times when I had just binged. And on days when I was not so sure about recovery, and I started out the day by skipping meals, it was hard to figure out how to stay on track.

We were also supposed to keep track of what we ate and when, and whether or not we compensated with eating-disordered behaviors. I was able to spot a major pattern within a few weeks – I would tell myself I did not need a whole meal, so I would try to have just a 'bite' or a 'snack' of something. Then, I would have another, and maybe another couple bites of something else. Then, I would feel like crap, because I would think "Well, I am supposed to eat again soon, but I have probably eaten plenty of random bites, it could have been a meal." Finally, I realized that I was doing the random-bites-of-everything thing at almost the EXACT times I was actually scheduled to eat a meal!

So my next goal was to start eating actual meals (the first step focused more on timing, not the composition of meals). I started trying to eat a balance of carbohydrates, protein, and fat at every meal, with snacks in between.

During this time, I found myself dealing with incredible amounts of hunger. It was like once my body tasted real food again, it would not stop asking for more. I remember so many times when I had just eaten a full meal, and I was still hungry. I would tell myself just to go hungry, but then I would feel like crap. So I would eat. And I would hate that I had to eat more, but I would feel better for a moment. Then, sometimes as little as a half hour later, I would be really hungry again. I would literally cry and scream and get so upset and say, "Why am I hungry? I do no WANT to be hungry!"

During this time, I gained a lot of weight, too fast for my taste. I felt awful. I looked awful. I could not move the same. My skin itched from stretching so fast. I was really constipated. I would get dizzy often. I would get horrible headaches, major blood sugar crashes, mood swings, night sweats, and so on. I would get horribly dehydrated. None of my clothes fit anymore. And since I lived in a downtown apartment by myself, I had no money to spend on clothes.

I felt like I wanted to wear a sign that said something like, "I am a recovering anorexic. Please do not think I got fat because I am just greedy and lazy." My anorexic mind was still very eating disordered, but my body no longer looked like it. THAT was hard.

My saving grace? A bunch of slobbery little two-year olds. Yes, I credit the initial stages of my recovery to a group of two-year olds. There were so many days where I woke up and just wanted to be invisible. I felt like everyone would stare at me, point, and laugh and make fun of me. I felt like my friends would be disgusted. I felt like people would stop being nice to me on the street. I was terrified at how people would react to my ever-expanding backside.

But every day, when I walked into that classroom, **there was not a single little person who cared about what I looked like.** All they cared about was that I was there to play with them, read them stories, and give them hugs. And they gave me lots of hugs, too! It was really a powerful thing to realize that through the unbiased eye of a toddler, my body was irrelevant. **My soul was what mattered.** Not only that, but working at a daycare also meant that the kids were fed a balanced breakfast, lunch, and snack every day. I started to take advantage of the pre-planned, balanced meals at 'normal' times.

The more I ate at meals, the less I binged. However, for a very long time, I was still incredibly hungry. I never felt satisfied. Sometimes I would swear I was not hungry at all, but when I finally ate something, I would realize that I was actually starving.

I was not really sure how much I should be eating. I literally had no clue what I needed. I wanted to see a nutritionist so bad but could not really afford one. I spent hours and hours looking for research studies, reading nutrition textbooks, studying physiology, etc. But still, I felt like I was not sure what to do. And my eating habits reflected that. I was eating more and feeling better – less cold, less tired, a bit more awake, a bit more **alive** – and I was actually engaged in conversations *and in life.*

The first weekend of April, the UofM hockey team competed in the National Championship tournament that just happened to be held right here in St Paul. As I rode the bus with the other cheerleaders and the band to the XCel Energy Center, I turned around in my seat and saw a cute boy behind me. We bonded over our similar experience teaching, just getting out of a serious relationship (me calling off my wedding, him going through with a marriage then divorcing very shortly after). A friend of mine was dating his friend, so I asked if she could figure out if he had a girlfriend. He did. So I decided to give up on the boy. That was on Thursday (the semi-final game). Then, when we rode the same bus on Saturday, his friend informed me that he had just broken up with his girlfriend the night he met me. I was a bit freaked out at how quickly he broke it off with her, and then he told me, "When you meet the right girl and you know it, why stay with one that's already not going well?" That night, we won the National Championship game. The entire city went crazy. There was rioting everywhere. Justin and I stayed up the whole night talking. We have been dating ever since.

So where am I going with this? When Justin met me, I had gained some weight (but not much compared to what I would still gain). I was a cute little cheerleader when we met. One month later, I had gained a good amount of weight. I made the mistake of trying to dye my hair blonde (I am definitely a brunette for life now!), and cutting it short. None of my clothes fit, and I had no real money to spend on clothes. I ended up wearing some really old 'fat pants,' some super-cheap things I got on clearance, and some awful, awful jeans that I swear were from the seventies. I felt so ugly. My new short haircut only accentuated my now-chubby cheeks.

But Justin did not care. He absolutely refused to make any comments about my weight, and he wiped my tears when I had a meltdown about gaining weight. He did not understand, but he just told me that he was not going anywhere just because of my weight. Of course, I was terrified. I figured it was only a matter of time before he finally got sick of me and left. I told myself that I needed to lose weight as soon as possible, or he would never want to stay with me.

Around this time, I settled into a regular pattern of eating at regular meal times, but eating just a little bit less than I really should have, so I would be very hungry before the next meal. Then I would eat, but still try to be hungry when I stopped, figuring this would help me lose weight.

I was completely wrong. I kept gaining. I would cry day after day, I would cry about how I was restricting and I felt like crap but I kept right on gaining. This went on for a few months, until finally, one day, I gave in. I could not fight the weight gain anymore. The restriction was not working anymore. I decided to just go ahead and eat whenever I wanted to. The week I finally did this, I lost a bit of weight. I was completely, totally shocked. A few weeks after that – this is maybe at the end of July, beginning of August of that year, about six months after I started recovery – I was eating a meal and suddenly I realized, **I am satisfied. I can stop now**.

It was almost too wonderful to be real. I finally felt satisfied, and I knew that I had just eaten a normal meal. Words cannot describe the level of elation I felt at that moment. It was the first time I had felt 'satisfied' after a meal for, oh, I do not even know how long. Years! I literally cried tears of joy.

About five months into my recovery, I felt physically better, as in more energetic, more alert, less cold, less anxious and irritable. I still found myself talking incessantly about how I was going to 'fix' my body through exercise and eating so and so and such things like that. My poor Justin, I did not even realize until now just how incredibly patient he was back then.

I had this issue of never wanting to eat a full-size meal. By now I could eat, no problem. But I did not want to finish an adult-size portion in one sitting. I could even eat most of the meal, then return for the rest perhaps an hour later. Weird, I know. But that was a rule that I was still in the process of breaking.

Six months into recovery, I was much larger than I would have been comfortable with before. And I learned that when you put on weight fairly quickly, it does not just automatically look like a 'normal' body shape. I have always (just like everyone in my family) gained all my weight in my butt and thighs. But during recovery, for the first time ever, I gained a bunch of weight around my stomach. I had NEVER worried about my stomach before! In time, the weight redistributed itself, and I look just fine now. But at the time, I was extremely uncomfortable. I had also gained quite a bit on my inner thighs, and I found it difficult to cross my legs. When I went running, my upper thighs would get red and raw and bleed just from my legs rubbing together. I hated it.

The thing about eating disorders is that your main goal is to get through today by holding on to whatever small comfort you can find. And hiding behind a bony body brought some strange kind of security and sense of satisfaction. Feeling numbed-out and distanced from everything brings a weird sort of comfort. Feeling dizzy and fuzzy-headed all the time provides a sort of defense against really experiencing anything at all.

The problem was, even though my mind was very much eating disordered still, my body no longer represented that. And I felt like a freak. But eventually, I got to a point where I was like, "Okay, nothing I do today is going to make me a skinny anorexic by the end of the day. It is my choice whether or not I will sit at home and cry about that, or whether I will do my best to go out and try to enjoy myself." So I started searching for joy in things OTHER than my physical self. I reached out to old friends whom I had alienated myself from. I tried new hobbies. I spent a lot of time really focusing on LIVING.

The interesting part?

My friends welcomed me back with open arms. My illness had put distance between us. My illness had made me so incredibly self-centered – I was constantly thinking about my weight, my body, calories, food – that I could not even take five minutes to really focus on any REAL conversation with anyone. I was so stressed by my own issues that I could not be supportive of my friends. I was too tired to go out. That all changed when I was in recovery.

Suddenly, it was extremely important to me to really get to know who my friends were. I actually found myself in a vulnerable position – something I have always done my best to avoid at all costs! And I was pleasantly surprised to experience just how concerned my friends were about my mental well-being. And how little they cared about my body. As one friend of mine put it, "When you were sick, it was like you were not there. You were not the friend I knew. You were just a lump of negativity. Now, you are vibrant. You are energetic, engaging, caring, fun, friendly, open, and interested in what's going on around you."

Justin and I spent the summer taking little 'mini-adventures' every chance we got. We would spend the day bike riding in a state park, or we would go to some very weird restaurant where we could not pronounce anything on the menu. We watched parades and visited friends and met family and went places and traveled and just, in general, LIVED.

By the end of summer, I had shed some weight, not by trying! I had continued to eat just as I had done before. In fact, I think I ate MORE than I had before. *The fun part?* I barely noticed the weight loss. **I did not care.** My life, for the first time in a very, very long time, was full. I did not have a need that was not met on some level – I had friends, hobbies, a great place to live, a boyfriend who loved me, my health, happiness, and a future to look forward to. I was back in school and I could finally concentrate again. I was taking classes in neurochemistry and anatomy and sports psychology and loving every bit of it. No more staring blankly at the page, waiting for the fuzziness to clear for a second so I could try to make sense of the words, only to forget them seconds later.

I finally, finally, finally felt ALIVE.

And 'alive' is a very GOOD way to feel.

Joy Nollenberg is thirty years old and lives in Minnesota. She struggled with eating disorders for thirteen years and is now recovered. Joy is the founder of *The Joy Project*, a non-profit organization that raises eating disorder awareness. For more information about *The Joy Project* and to get in touch with Joy, go to www.joyproject.org

This poem is an interaction between me and my eating disorder (the skeleton). It felt very liberating to write the poem and was my way of formally saying goodbye to the former ideas I had about food intake and body image.

The Skeleton

By Theresa Grimsley

The skeleton visited last night in my dreams.
It sat before me, strung out on coffee and laxatives
Apologizing yet again for the hurt it caused me.
This time I hardly listened and felt only annoyance
At seeing it again, old and weak.
No strength there that I could see.
It was dead and had no idea.

The skeleton laughed a few times about things we shared in the past
Like how much fun it was to not eat when we drank
And how I always ended up with my head in the toilet
Swearing I would never drink again or begging God to kill me.
Fun times.
The skeleton and me.

I sat upright before the skeleton, happy that I had curves
Happy that my belly was comfortable... not too full and not too hungry
Or contorting inside like an angry cat begging for a morsel.
I knew what the skeleton felt, because I was close to it once.
It smiled at me but the smile never reached its sunken eyes
And I knew that the skeleton hated me for being healthy,
Yet yearned for exactly that.

I watched the skeleton play its game, or at least attempt to,
But its words were mere sounds, like waves on the ocean.
I did not attempt to make sense of them, only listened to the rhythm.
Then, with a sigh, I stood.
Surprise passed the skeleton's ashen face.
"Are you leaving?" it asked.
"I left a long time ago," I answered.

Theresa Grimsley is thirty-three years old and lives in the United States. Theresa is married and has two sons. She struggled with anorexia and bulimia for over fifteen years and is now in recovery.

My Eaters Agreement

By Reema Arora

I, Reema Arora, agree to live in a passionate and juicy way instead of just merely existing like I have for the last seven years. I will continue to nourish my mind, body, and soul and never allow deprivation to be a part of my life ever again. I will honor my needs and fulfill my desires with the knowledge that I am truly worth it. I will know that I am special and unique and that my eating disorder was never who I was as a person. It was only a struggle that I was meant to go through in this life that has made me stronger, allowed me to discover my soul self, and taught me valuable life lessons.

I agree to treat my body like the holy temple that it was meant to be and accept that I am a picture of true beauty because God created me. I agree to always know that I am not a forgotten smudge on God's canvas but an essential part of his world design. I will never again attempt to starve myself down to nothingness because the end result is a tortured soul and a suffocated spirit**. I agree to actively take up space, embrace my inner strength, and become a defining presence in this world.** My body will shake with genuine laughter, my eyes will sparkle with mischief, and my lips will never again be denied the sweet taste of chocolate.

I agree to use my voice. I will speak my needs and defend my beliefs. I will stand up for myself and be just as fiercely protective of myself as I would be for any of those people whom I love. I agree to be more selfish sometimes because taking care of me will from now on always be one of my top priorities. Instead of stuffing down my feelings, I will speak my truth and never allow my soul to be stifled again. I agree to take the amazing determination, strength, and pure stubbornness I have used to flourish in my eating disorder and redirect it to achieving my dreams in life. I will continue to shoot for the moon, but I will now know that even if I don't get there, I will always lie amongst the stars.

I agree to acknowledge my fears of growing up and striving for independence. I will face those fears head on by using the strength I now know I have, leaning on the people I know are supporting me, and having faith that I will overcome any obstacles set in my way. I agree to travel by taxi every now and then, because even though I know how unreliable they are, I know that I will eventually reach my home because I will somehow always find my way. I am not a damsel in distress, and my identity is not one of fragility. I am from this day forward a girl who has realized her inner goddess.

I agree to continue to accept my body more and more each and every day. I may not yet look at myself in adoration but someday I will love myself because I will accept that my flaws are what make me beautifully human. I will no longer chase after unreachable ideals or support the unreasonable expectation of perfection. My purpose on earth is not to destroy myself because I don't measure up to some ridiculous unknown and unwritten standards. My purpose is to treat myself with love and respect, experience deep meaningful connections with other souls, do my part to better the planet in some tiny way, and live out all of my wildest dreams.

I agree to live in the present moment. I will not spend time regretting the past or trying to manipulate the future. I will live for today because Kal Ho Na Ho, Tomorrow May Not Come. I agree to walk with my head held up high and to smile at strangers that pass me by because I am sick of putting all of my energy into shrinking into an invisible speck on the sidewalk. I agree to follow my heart and trust my instincts. I will wake up early to watch the sun rise and go to bed early when my body is calling for rest. I agree to ask for help when I need it instead of burning myself out by trying to do it all on my own. I agree to be who I am instead of staring in the mirror for hours trying to use all of my will power to somehow magically transform the image that stares back at me. I will try my hardest not to constantly compare myself to other women because for all I know they are actually comparing themselves to me. I will not contribute to the self-critical place that society has stuffed women into anymore.

I agree never to take life for granted ever again. I will celebrate every breath I take and cherish each moment spent on this planet earth. I will never again numb myself against pain or difficult emotions because the only way to experience true joy is if you have experienced deep sadness. I will not shy away from making my own decisions when it comes to choosing different paths in life because I now know that my heart will always lead me to exactly where I am meant to be. God has a beautiful destiny in mind for my journey in life but he has given me all the power, because it is only through my choices that I will be able to reach it. And the choice I am making now is for recovery, because that is the only way that I will ever make it to the beautiful life that is intended to be my fate.

I agree to continue on my journey to recovery no matter how hard it may be or how daunting the long road in front of me is. Although the uncertainty of my future scares me, I agree to walk forward into it without ever looking back. And when my mind tries to glorify the disordered past I am leaving behind, I will read my journals that I have kept here to remind myself of all the pain and heartache that my family and I have had to go through in order to leave that very same past behind. I agree to be totally honest and I will voice my struggles and admit my slips, because that is the only way that I will ever truly make it out of this disorder. I agree to someday completely listen to my body which means to eat when I am hungry, stop when I am full, and indulge when something is yummy. I agree to someday let go of measuring myself by any sort of number, may it be the number on the scale or the size on a label of a pair of pants. I will be one more woman in a revolution to love and accept ourselves just the way we are.

I agree to have a banana split on banana split day at work, even if I have already had my lunch. I agree to eat a turkey burger at a barbeque with my future boyfriend, yes I do mean a burger bun, not chopped up indistinguishable goulash. I agree to sometimes drink a glass of juice instead of having a piece of fruit. I agree to eat a spontaneously desired concoction while standing up next to a food stall at a village fair. I agree to grab a protein bar and eat it in my car if I need to, because from now on food will be scheduled into my life instead of my life being scheduled around my food. And I definitely agree to have a piece of cake on my wedding day and have the leftovers for breakfast the next morning.

I relinquish my eating disorder. I release basing my self-worth on the visibility of my bones. I release believing that starving myself down to my tiniest form possible and surviving on as little as possible is what makes me special in this world. I release my refusal to believe that I have good qualities and am a worthy individual. I release the walls I have created to surround myself and isolate me from the life that is happening around me. I release being my harshest critic and focusing on all of my flaws. I release the part of me that wants to lie and manipulate to perpetuate a disorder that was causing me to slowly die. I release using disordered behaviors to cope with life and numb myself into another safer world. I release the thought that life is not worth fighting for because the life I have been having is definitely not the one I want for myself. I release existing as a tortured soul in a starving body.

I relinquish the Me I thought I was and agree to continue my journey towards health, love, and true happiness because I realize that my ideal of perfection does not exist and that I am now and forever will be a beautiful work in progress.

Reema Arora is a medical student living in Chicago, Illinois.

"I am not 'anorexic.' In fact, I never was… I am a girl who has struggled with Anorexia Nervosa.

"I was utterly entrenched in my eating disorder for seven years, and have been actively pursuing my recovery for the last two years. At the age of twenty-seven, after taking four years off after college because of my illness and various inpatient treatments, I have finally achieved my life-long goal of attending medical school.

"My desire to be a physician was actually the only thing that kept me going a lot of the time; having a dream about what I wanted my contribution to this earth to be. And to be honest, a big part of me had started believing that I would never make it because I did not think I would be able to sustain a lasting recovery. But here I am, coming close to completing my first year! The best part of achieving my dream is in knowing that the kind of physician I am going to be, and the way in which I will practice medicine in the future, have been molded and reshaped by the struggles I have gone through. My perspective on the world has been altered, the compassion for others within my heart has grown, and my respect for the human spirit and journey has become my guiding forces.

"How did I get here? I closed my eyes, crossed my fingers, and jumped.... holding on to my faith that the other side would be as beautiful as I hoped it would be. It was hard work to let go of the one thing I held as sacred, the disorder that became my identity and comfort, the very thing that I was sure was keeping me afloat. Even after two years, it is still difficult at times to truly feel my sadness, experience my anger, sit in my loneliness, and acknowledge my doubts and insecurities. But I have decided that life is worth fighting for. Because even when it is really really hard… life is still pretty spectacular!

"I believe full recovery is possible with all of my heart, and I know that one day I will get there – but I also know the only person who can get me there is me. The choice is mine, the hard work is mine, and the determination to keep walking forward is mine.

"The message I want to give you is this: You are way more than you know yourself to be. So cross your fingers, hold onto your faith, recognize your inner strength, and take your first step forward."

Poems by Johnie Drew

I wrote this at the beginning of my recovery when I realized that I really could recover. It was possible. And I could do it. I was strong enough to beat my disease.

Strong Enough

Strong enough to stand up and fight.
Strong enough to see the light.

Strong enough to ask for help when it is in need.
Strong enough to make the commitment to recovery and succeed.

Strong enough to disagree with Ed and say NO!
Strong enough to allow a new person to emerge and grow.

Strong enough to overcome all the obstacles in my way.
Strong enough to know that my worth is not measured by what I weigh.

Strong enough to love me and gain self-esteem.
Strong enough to know with Ed things are not always how they seem.

Strong enough to do the next right think I know I should do.
Strong enough to get back up no matter what I may go through.

Strong enough to withstand each storm.
Strong enough to change my life and transform.

Strong enough to see the future and the life that could be.
Strong enough to know that will one day be me.

Strong enough to hear my own voice.
Strong enough to see that I do have a choice.

I am stronger than I ever knew I could be.
I am strong enough to set myself free.

This poem is all about how Ed (eating disorder) makes me do dumb things all the time when the real me knows better. It is about me questioning how Ed is so powerful.

How Can I?

How can I see so well, but be so blind?
How can I love adventure, but allow myself to be confined?
How can I hate liars, but listen to one everyday?
How can I be so wise, but be ruled by what I weigh?
How can I be such a positive person, but also so negative?
How can I love life so much, but continue each day not to live?
How can I be such a health nut, but do things that are so bad for me?
How can I know Ed is wrong, but still not disagree?
How can I be so educated, but so ignorant at the same time?
How can I have such great faith, but not see any of the signs?
How can I be so strong, but when I fall not push through?
How can I know in my heart there is only one God, but still worship two?
How can I have such a big heart, but have no love for myself at all?
How can I stand up to anyone or anything, but allow Ed to make me feel so small?
How does Ed do it?
This I do not get?
How does he completely change the people we are?
And how does it get so far?
This mystery I will never understand.
But I do understand this is not what I had planned.
I do still know who I truly am inside.
And I know that girl is still alive, she has not died.
So I will let the awakening begin.
And I know in the end even if I do not know the answers to these questions I will still win.

This poem is about jumping and leaping into recovery and trusting it. Trusting that you can get well and live a life full of happiness if you just jump.

JUMP

Take the leap of faith, Jump of that cliff
No conditions, No what ifs
Trust in yourself, Trust in God
No more pretending, No more fake facade
Your life without Ed is waiting, and it is worth it
Do not look back, Do not quit
Once you jump it will be a new dawn
You will have something solid to stand on
Or you will learn how to fly
Then you can start living, and tell Ed good-bye.
So run, jump, leap, or skip
Do what ever it takes to get off that cliff

I wrote this poem for my husband in the beginning of my recovery when things were crazy and I was starting to realize how much my disease had cost me. And sometimes it is hard for me to express my emotions because of my disease and with this poem he will always know how I feel.

I am Sorry – Thank you – I love you

I am sorry for the pain my disease has caused you.
I know it makes you frustrated and sad too.
I am sorry for being so disconnected.
I know I have not been very loving and affectionate.
I am most sorry for letting Ed come between you and me.
I know you wish for us both to one day be free.

I thank you for staying by my side.
For coming along this crazy ride.
I thank you for all the help and support you give.
For helping me get by each day and live.
I thank you most of all for being patient and loving me.
One day we WILL be free.

I love you and appreciate all you do.
I love everything little thing about you.
I love the way you live life.
And I love being your wife.
I love how we compliment and complete each other.
And I could never see myself with another.

© Johnie Drew

This is about all the steps – the good, the bad, and the ugly – that we take in recovery.

Steps

We take steps each day towards recovery
Each step is different and full of discovery

Some steps are very small
Some are just a baby's crawl

Some steps are a huge leap
Some we may take in our sleep

Some steps can cause great pain
Some can make us feel insane

Some steps take us through valleys and over hills
Some can teach us new skills

Some steps are so scary we cannot even look
Some we do not even realize we took

Some steps make us very sad
Some we have to take make us mad

Some steps can make us smile
Some make all our time and energy worthwhile

Some steps make us glad when they are done
Some make us want to turn around and run

Some steps make us very proud
Some we must take through a rain cloud

Some steps we feel like we continue to repeat
And then sometimes we do not want to take any steps and just rest our feet

No matter the step, great or small
Each step matters, we must take them all

Everyone's steps are different, there are no guarantees
But each step is one closer to setting yourself free

So keep taking each step and make your own trail
And remember to just keep putting one foot in front of the other and you will prevail.

I attended the 'Divorcing Ed' weekend retreat given by Thom Rutledge and Jenni Schafer**. It was a wonderful experience... I learned a lot of valuable information. So when I got home, I wrote a poem summarizing everything that I had learned so I would not forget any of it.*

Willing To Do Whatever It Takes

Work at it daily. This will take lots of practice.
Inside yourself find your inner parent.
Let it all go. Just let it go!
Learn self-compassion. You cannot do this without it.
Isolate and separate yourself from Ed, not your loved ones.
No Conditions! You cannot have any!
Give your attention to your Recovery Voice, not ED.

Tackle issues with distorted body image-be curious.
Obtain your own value system and stick with it.

Depend on and Trust God! Keep the Faith!
Own your Recovery! It is your responsibility.

Weight will fluctuate – you have to allow this to happen.
Have in mind that this is a long and very tough journey.
Ask yourself: What do I want? How do I feel?
Trust others opinions, not yours or Eds.
Eat Healthy – do not deprive, restrict, or abuse food.
Volunteer for the pain. There will be lots of it.
Exercise Healthy – do not abuse this either.
Remember recovery is possible, it does happen.

Implement your support system when needed.
Think about how irrational Ed is – he is a LIAR!

Take baby steps each day. If you fall down get back up!
Acknowledge your own progress in recovery.
Kiss perfectionism good-bye. Nobody is perfect.
Express your feelings in any way needed.
Scream "Screw you, Ed!" loudly and often. It helps!

Johnie Drew is twenty-seven years old, married and lives in Tennessee. She has struggled with her eating disorder for twenty years and is now in recovery.

*For more information about Thom Rutledge, visit www.thomrutledge.com

**Jenni Schaefer's recovery story is also in this book.

Have you ever wanted to kick your eating disorder out of your life for good? You are not alone.

My Divorce Letter to My Eating Disorder

By Mary Pat Nally

Dear Eating Disorder,

It has been a tough couple weeks. I am tired; exhausted, actually. I feel as though my strength is gone. I have been thinking about how long we have been together. When I think about it, I get frustrated, angry, discouraged, and empty.

I met you when I was in the sixth grade. You wanted to be my friend when no one else would. You helped me with Math and spelling. Anorexia, bulimia and compulsive overeating. You said, number one: Do not trust anyone because they will end up hurting or leaving you. Number two: Do not tell anyone anything because they really do not care anyway. Number three: Feelings are to be kept to yourself.

You have saved me from conflict, kept me focused, helped me become independent, and kept me safe. You also kept me from forming relationships, you controlled me, you told me that the numbers on the scale was all that mattered. You were mean to me, and you also allowed others to be mean to me. I was not strong enough to tell them to stop.

You taught me to hate my body, to despise everything about it. You said my hair was too curly, my shoulders were too broad, my breasts were too big, my thighs were too fat, my stomach needed to be cut out, and my calves were just huge. You convinced me that no man would ever find me attractive and that the world would be better off if I were invisible.

I appreciate you taking care of me when I needed you, but **I do not need you anymore**. I have been running from you for the past twelve years and wherever I go, there you are, ready, willing and waiting. I have gone as far away as Alaska to try to get rid of you. I jumped out of a plane five thousand feet in the air, climbed thirty feet in the air and walked along a cable – both things I did trying to get rid of you.

You told me that people would not want me around unless I was being of service and forgot about myself. Some days you even tried to get me to stay in bed and not go to work. That did not work because you were sending me mixed messages. On one hand you told me to stay in bed, but on the other hand you told me that I had to be the perfect teacher. You did not care that it was my first year. You told me to get up at 4:30 am to work on my lesson plans; you let my kids walk all over me. For nine years of my life you had me running away from myself. You told me that I did not need God, and sometimes I actually believed you.

When I started teaching you tried to tell me that God did not matter, that sleep was more important. I have God on my side at church. I ignored you. I put my heart into my singing. I also started to form relationships with others and stayed in one place for a year. You hated that! You wanted me all to yourself.

I was not strong enough to keep you away. My confidence was shot, and I was afraid of people. You told me I looked like a kid and that adults were never going to accept me. You said that men would never find me attractive. You made me afraid of myself, never comfortable in my own skin. You told me I was short, fat, and ugly, and I believed you.

You should be ashamed of yourself, ruining my life like that. I am putting in for a divorce and taking you to court. You are being sued for personality theft, personal damages, and I am getting sole custody of myself. You have no visitation rights – if you try to visit, I will be ready. I might not be strong now, but the people around me are helping me become strong. They love me; they believe in me, they value my presence on this earth.

You have destroyed too many lives.
I am no longer running, *I am sitting.*
I am not doing, *I am being.*
I am not dying, *I am rising.*
I am no longer fake, *I am real.*
I am no longer ashamed of myself, *I am proud.*
I am no longer dead, *I am alive.*
Together we will become strong
and put you in your place.

Mary Pat Nally is thirty-eight years old and lives in Ventura County, California. She has her Masters Degree in Spiritual Psychology and has recovered/healed from twenty-four years of eating disordered behaviors. She is the founder of *Learn, Lead and Serve*, whose mission is to provide a space where students of all ages have the opportunity to become their authentic selves. She is a mentor and recovery coach for others who are walking their own healing journey. She is the author of *Reflecting Grace* and is currently working on her second book. Mary Pat is available for speaking and workshop engagements throughout the United States and Canada. For more information and to get in touch with Mary Pat, visit www.authenticallyme.com

Have you ever wanted to kill your eating disorder? I did. To dwell on the negative keeps me feeling bad, so I work on seeing how my eating disorder has blessed me...

Ten Ways My Eating Disorder Has Blessed My Life

1. I get a second chance to love.
2. I am able to truly enjoy and appreciate every day.
3. My life is NEVER boring.
4. If I missed a lesson the first time around, I know I will get another chance.
5. My life has become true experiential education – learning by doing.
6. I have learned that my body is absolutely amazing.
7. I have met, and continue to meet, amazing individuals who change my perspective on how I see the world.
8. I am alive and able to impact the lives of others by sharing my own experiences.
9. I have been able to strengthen my spirituality.
10. I have learned each human being is beautiful in his or her own way.

© Mary Pat Nally

The Power of Eating Disorders

I want to get close
I am afraid.
Afraid of what you might see.
My eyes.
My thoughts.
My dreams.
My heart.
My soul.
Everything that makes me who I am.
My feelings.
My emotions.
The truth of my own reality.
The reality that I am scared.
Every second.
Every minute.
Every hour.
Every day.
Scared of not being perfect.
Scared of looking stupid.
Scared of being in the way.
Scared of getting comfortable.
Getting comfortable means stability,
Stability means forever.
I dread forever.
So, I am ready, to move on,
to continue my journey,
To continue my life....
I AM READY!

Aphrodite

"Aphrodite, the Goddess of Love in Greek mythology, is born out of sea foam. In the midst of a wild storm, rays of sunlight pierce through dark clouds. The sky reveals the face of Mary. Even when her face is hidden, may you reach towards her light."

'Coming Home' is a series if three drawings that depict the process of healing and coming into harmony with the body

Coming Home # 1: Hatred

"Often we live in our heads, cut off and separated from the body. Such a woman projects hatred and disgust onto her body. Inside a closed shell in her belly is an angry child who never receives any attention."

Coming Home # 2: Grief

"As she begins to turn her attention into her body, she discovers the pain of long buried wounds. Inside her belly, an adolescent girl huddles in an effort to protect herself. This willingness to feel again and to grieve begins a process of self-awareness and self-kindness, thus the shell begins to open. Her hands reach down and caress the parts that have been neglected for so long… reconnecting brings wholeness."

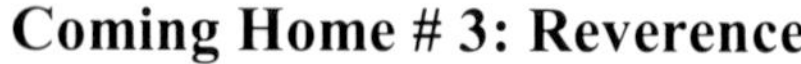

Coming Home # 3: Reverence

"Here the light of awareness floods into her body. Inside is a fully-grown woman, as Venus on the open shell represents her newly discovered beauty. Although her body stays the same shape, there is an acceptance and appreciation for her unique form."

Robin Maynard-Dobbs is a personal coach and founder of *Aware Eating*. She has been helping women successfully overcome compulsive eating since 1991. Robin offers a unique and holistic approach to recovery from eating disorders and obsession with food / weight. Through mindfulness, Robin guides women to connect and respond to their bodies with kindness.

As women let go of judgment, they learn how to eat naturally, and to care for their bodies with honor and respect. For many years, Robin was driven by compulsive overeating followed by excessive exercise so she knows firsthand the process of recovery from an eating disorder. As she now lives in joy and harmony with her body, she is freed up to pursue her passion of helping other women overcome their struggle with food. Inspired by a lifelong meditation practice, she teaches others to look inside themselves for the wisdom they seek. Based in Seattle, Washington, Robin is available either in person or coaching over the phone. For more information about Robin and her work and to sign up for a free half hour initial consultation, visit www.awareeating.com

My Story

By J. J. S.

My mind would repeat the same few sentences as I raced up the stairs every evening after dinner. "Lock the door. Turn on the water. Vomit. Vomit until your eyes are red, your chest hurts, your throat burns, and you are certain, absolutely certain, that everything is out of your stomach. You are not good enough. You are too fat. Too ugly. Too un-perfect."

I knew what I was doing, I knew that I was performing a slow suicide on myself on a daily basis, but I did not care. I needed to be more than who I was, and believed being thin was going to get me there.

I do not remember the first time I felt fat or that I was not good enough. I remember the exact time and place I first made myself throw up my dinner. I remember what I thought afterwards, and I remember how I felt, but I do not remember when being the person I was, was not who I thought I should be.

I was nine-years old, and doing a school project at a friend's house. We could not get our model cactus to look exactly how we imagined it to be, and I was frustrated with myself. We had been trying to get our desert to duplicate the picture we had and our cactus just did not look like a cactus. We were angry, but I was taking it a little more personal I think because I had chosen that picture to model our desert on.

Then my friend's mom came into her bedroom and told us that dinner was ready. I do not know what made me decide that I needed to throw up, but I went in to her bathroom, and stuck my finger down my throat and watched the food come back up and into the toilet. I felt so much better. I felt as if finally, I had got something right.

This was not something I did every day from that point on; it was something I did when I did not get the right grade on a Math test, or when I did not say the right thing and I got into an argument with my mom. It was my way of punishing myself for my mistakes. Then, suddenly, one day a few years later, I stopped just as quickly as I had started.

In my junior year I started dating this guy from another school. James* was the same age as me. He had blonde hair and blue eyes. He was a swimmer and a baseball player so he had an athlete's body. He was great!

The first time we met we hit it off instantly. My friends were not so excited for me though. They knew him and warned me about his constant lying and occasional temper. But he was my first boyfriend, so I was excited and would not listen to my friends' warnings. After a few weeks I caught him in his first lie. Some of the girls at my church, who went to school with James, told me he was bragging about having sex with his new girlfriend and asked me if it were true. I told them the truth – we were not having sex. When we talked later that night I told him what was said, and he told me that it was just a rumor, he would have told people the truth if it had gotten back to him. I believed him. Why would he lie to me?

A few months went by, and James started treating me a little differently. He started yelling at me in the car when I was singing too loud or talking too much or not talking enough or disagreeing with him. Anything he could yell at me for he was taking the chance to do so. I started getting angry and yelling back. He hated that I was standing up for myself. One night, I must have yelled a little too much because he grabbed my face, told me to shut up, and kind of pushed me back away from him. I was so angry and scared that I did not talk to him for a few days. Finally, after enough phone calls begging me to forgive him, I started seeing him again.

The summer of my senior year it seemed like everything was going wrong. My home life was worse than ever with everyone constantly fighting. I felt as though I was the cause of all the problems. My brother and sister would always tell me that nobody fought when I was not around. So I truly believed I caused my family member's anger and frustration towards one another. I felt ignored and unwanted.

That summer, my grandmother, who had been my best friend in the entire world, was diagnosed with colon cancer. Three weeks later, my grandfather had to have quadruple bypass surgery. I was so afraid I would lose both of them but I did not know how to keep them safe, so I started running to get my mind off the thought of losing my grandparents. Running turned into joining a gym, which turned into dancing, which turned into exercising for numerous hours a day and, eventually, restricting calories. By the time my senior year had come I had lost quite a few pounds. It was not drastic, but it was enough for someone to notice.

Lunch time at school was terrible. I did not know what to do to prevent my friends from staring at my abnormal eating habits and questioning me with each bite I was forcing down. One of the girls I ate lunch with had written a warning referral about me and gave it to the SAP (Student Assistance Program) Team and so I had teachers watching me at lunch. On the days that I would eat more than a few bites, I would go to the bathroom to rid my body of calories. It worked for a while until a teacher would follow me and stay in the bathroom until after I left. After a few weeks, the same teacher, whom I had for class later that day, told me that she had a sister with an eating disorder and that she was concerned. After that, I started skipping my lunch period and doing work in the student council room. That worked until the principal started calling, looking for me and wondering why I was not eating.

When my grandma died I completely lost it. I started binging and purging a couple of times a day. I would hide my vomit in big zip-lock baggies until I could get rid of it without anyone knowing. I would go running and detour into the woods to throw up. When I started throwing up blood it did not scare me, but I knew that I needed to stop before I damaged my body anymore. The only problem was, I did not know how to stop, and I felt like I could not tell anybody about what I was doing. I was slowly not only physically wasting away, I was mentally deteriorating as well.

After my grandma passed away, James decided to be nice for a while. We were getting along great until one night, a few months later, he got some of our friends together and we all went out for dinner and a movie. I played with my food more than I ate it. While we were eating, he told me that he had decided to take another girl to the prom, not me. I was so upset I started to cry. This was our senior year, and I was his girlfriend and I reserved the right to go with him to his prom as he was coming to my prom. The waitress came over to ask if we needed anything, and because James worked at the restaurant we were in, she knew him and asked if I was okay. He said, "Yeah, she's my girlfriend and is just being selfish."

This upset me even more. I excused myself and went to the bathroom to purge the few bites of what I had eaten and went to sit outside. The whole way to the movies he argued with me, trying to justify the prom situation. I was not giving in on this one. At the movies he kept trying to grab me and pinch my legs. He wanted to show that he had control over me. When I would not allow him to do this he got so mad he grabbed me and pulled me out of the theater and into his car where he started screaming at me. With every name he called me, he took more and more of my pride and self-respect away. When he was done with the verbal abuse we went back in to the theater.

I was not going to cry this time. I could not cry any more. He won when I cried. When the movie was over, the group decided to go to my school's annual volleyball marathon. We pulled into the parking lot and James kept me in the car. Our friends were not sure about leaving me there, but I assured them that I was going to be okay. However, as soon as they went inside, the fighting started all over again. This time I got out of the car, and as I did, James got out too and threw me up against the car and shoved me back inside. A few minutes later, my friends came out of the school, ready to go home.

It was almost midnight, but instead of taking us all home, James drove his car down a dirt road that led to a secluded spot in the woods. He parked his car, got his jacket, and started walking. We were all confused. After a few minutes, the two guys who were with us went to look for him, leaving my friend and me alone in the car. As she and I sat in silence for a few minutes, she asked if I thought James had a gun in his jacket. That thought had already run through my mind a thousand times, but when she said it, it made it real. We both knew he never wore a jacket, so why start now? I said that I did not know and it was quiet until she spoke again a few minutes later.

What she said next surprised me more than it should have. She told me that James had been cheating on me with her after school when he drove her home. I knew that she had liked him, but he promised me that nothing was going on. They were neighbors, and she was like his little sister. I felt so dumb for believing him. The guys came back to James' vehicle without him. They said he was okay and just needed some time to cool off. So we waited a few more minutes until he came back.

When he came back he looked at me with such hate in his eyes and then threatened me. At that moment, I was so numb – I forgot what it was like to feel. After that night and a bad breakup from James, it was not unusual for me to binge and purge more than I ever did before on a daily basis. I started taking numerous laxatives at a time and exercising for hours. I had totally secluded myself.

A few days later, a teacher I had had for English the year before asked me if I wanted to talk. I trusted her and could not keep my secret anymore. Deep down, I was afraid that I was going to die, either from what I was doing to myself, or what my boyfriend had been doing to me. So one afternoon, I stayed after school and after a while of small talk, I finally broke down and told her everything. I told her about having to always wear long sleeves to cover my bruises, but I still defended James by saying that he never hit me, which was true. He just pushed me around and grabbed me a lot. I told her about throwing up blood, my hair falling out and how I would exercise compulsively. I told her about how much weight I lost. I told her what it felt like to be me, whoever that was.

Never once did she judge me or get disgusted by what I was telling her. Finally, after a few hours of talking and crying, she gave me what I so badly needed, the biggest and warmest hug I have ever received. **For the**

first time in a long time, I felt loved. For the first time, in so long, I felt as though I had a friend in this world, and I felt as though I did not have to go through this life ashamed and on my own. For the first time ever, she gave me hope. For weeks after that I did not want to leave her classroom. Being there with her was the one place that I felt safe. She encouraged me to get help and to tell someone else, but I refused. I was not ready to let go of my disorder. I was not ready to let go of the only thing I had that comforted me.

Prom came, and I was getting ready with one of my best friends. My dress laced up the sides, and you had to adjust it to fit. I had had it altered three weeks prior, but that day it was falling off of me. Her mom told my friend that she did not realize exactly how much weight I had lost until she saw my ribs through my dress.

After I graduated from high school I still often talked to my former teacher. Finally, I decided to tell my friend. She had suspected and had confronted me about it numerous times. We went to the track to walk, but there was a sports team using it and so we just sat down in the grass and I started crying and for the first time said the words "eating disorder." Once I had said those two words out loud it became more real. I told two more people after that, another friend and the teacher who had been following me to the bathroom.

The summer after I graduated, I grew enough nerve to call my doctor. I was not sure that I was ready to tell him, so when he got on the phone to talk to me, I asked him how he treated an eating disorder. He told me to come to his office right then and there to talk to him. I would not, I could not; I did not have enough courage to face him at that particular moment. Instead, I made an appointment and went in and we talked.

He and two of the nurses in his office were so caring and were always there when I needed anything. They found a therapist about an hour away from where I lived. I would meet with her once a week, and we would talk about everything except what was causing me to purge. Every once in a while she would have me do worksheets in her office about feelings, but I always wrote that I was happy and I did not know what was causing me to do such harm to my body, just that I was to fat. However, I did tell her about my obsessive need to have things in my closet, pantry, and refrigerator organized, and she told me I was weird. After she made that comment, I felt as though she was always judging me, and so I stopped seeing her.

During the time I was not in therapy, James came back into my life. We went out a few times and things were okay. I wanted so badly to believe that he had changed. Then one night I went to his house, and while I was drinking a glass of soda I suddenly got this really weird feeling so I laid down on his couch. I must have passed out, because when I woke up he was trying to force himself on top of me. I pushed him off and went home. Nothing happened, thank goodness, but I had a terrible headache when I woke up, so I assumed I had either had a migraine or it was caused by restricting my food intake. I did not want to think or believe that he could have possibly used the date rape drug.

Soon after, I started drinking. It was not just a drink here or there, it was hard liquor every day. I knew that if I were intoxicated I could eat and throw up and blame it on the alcohol and nobody would question me. When I started blacking out and not remembering things, my friends had to fill me in on the night before. But soon, it was not just at night that I would drink. My roommate at the time laughed because I opened up a bottle of vodka at six am and drank before I went to work. Soon, I was told that this was a problem as well. To protect my eating disorder I created an online page in a community that was pro-eating disorder. I needed someone to tell me that what I was doing was the right thing. I was spiraling even more out of control in a disorder which I thought gave me control.

My doctor soon found a psychologist who specialized in treating eating disorders about an hour away from my home. I was scared to work with him because I knew that he could possibly be the answer to my problems, but the first time I talked to him I knew I was in the right place. After a few weeks, he contacted my family doctor and together they put me on Prozac. I was nervous about taking an anti-depressant and had a list of questions I wanted answered before I would agree to go on it. Finally, after they both had taken the time to answer my questions, I talked to my cousin's wife, who also had suffered from bulimia, as well as getting my eleventh grade English teachers input and decided to try it for a while. It helped me so much, but after a while I started skipping pills and semi-abusing other prescription pills instead, and I was right back to where I was before. Except this time I started cutting along with my eating disorder and drinking problem.

I was a total mess. I did not know what to do. I wanted it all to end, but I did not want to die. I had flashes of watching myself die somehow never once did I truly want to end my life. I knew that there were people who cared too much about me, and I knew that one day I could use my story to help someone else. So, I laid my life in God's hands and asked Him to please help me. I kept going to therapy and worked with a nutritionist for a while. I met other girls who suffered from the same problems I did and I talked to them. Every time I told someone my story, it made it more real to me. It made me feel like I was pulling the mask I hid behind everyday off my face a little more.

One day, the real me will be completely revealed.

I am not completely free from anorexia and bulimia but I strive to be. I know that it is a long hard road, but it's one I am willing to walk down for as long as I have to in order to reach the end. When I see myself falling back in to my old habits I tell someone immediately what I just did or what I am thinking of doing. **Verbalizing things means that there is someone to walk beside me in this.** It means that I am not alone.

My eating disorder made me unbearable. I would scream and yell at everyone. I would cry at the littlest of things. I would seclude myself for days. I could not stand looking at myself in the mirror. All I saw were flabby arms, huge thighs, and a fat face, yet this image I was seeing was totally distorted from what everyone else was seeing. Although I still have my days where I get frustrated trying on clothes, and I catch myself reading labels, I know that I never want to be back to where I was such a short time ago.

I consider myself one of the lucky ones. I am blessed to not have lost the battle with my eating disorder. I was given a great support team who are always there at any hour of the day when I need someone to talk to. They never let me wallow in my self-pity; they know where that gets me. Instead, they guide me to take action and encourage me to be healthy. I stopped reading beauty magazines and use my website to encourage girls to talk to someone, even if it is me, about what they are going through. I know what it is like to need someone to listen and understand. I stopped drinking. I do not even take medicine with alcohol in it. Although I am probably a little too cautious when it comes to dating, I know that I am worth more than what James made me feel. But most importantly, I am gaining self-esteem and getting my self-respect back.

I believe that everyone has the power to overcome their struggles and I wish you the absolute best of luck in your walk towards recovery.

J. J. S. is twenty-years old and lives in Pennsylvania. She is a recovering bulimic of eleven years with anorexic tendencies. She is a college student and majors in Human Services with her area of concentration in social work and hopes to become a therapist for eating disorders and give back to people what so many have helped give back to her. If you want to get in touch with her, feel free to send an email to jjs@youarenotalonebook.com

*Name has been changed to protect person's privacy.

I wrote this poem when I was watching my little sister, barely a teenager, waste away. I felt somewhat responsible for her borderline eating disorder behaviors.

A Poem To My Beautiful Sister

I wish I could show you what the mirror does not
It shows you a lie of your shape and your size
So you restrict what you eat
So the number on the scale does not rise.

You exercise for hours on end
You run and jump and twist and bend
You do numerous crunches, run a mile, then bike
Will this ever stop? Will this ever end?

You are so beautiful
I wish you could see
That I love you just the way you are
You are absolutely perfect to me.

I feel so responsible
For what you are doing to yourself
I wish you could see
What you are doing to your health.

Why could not you have picked something else
That you admired in me
Not the way I deal with pain
Just let that part be.

I am so afraid for you sis,
You're getting so small

Even your friends cannot recognize you
As you walk down the hall

You are withering away
Get better, please try
If you do not
I am afraid that you're going to die.

This is a song that I wrote about myself when I was afraid of recovery but I needed it so badly.

My Song

She flushes her day away,
A day full of pain.
Happiness, attention, and love
Is the only thing she wants to gain.

What made her this way?
She keeps it inside,
A secret that's kept,
Away from the world she'll hide.

The abuse, the scars, the words, the tears.
No one loves her so what does it matter?
She looks in the mirror and hates who she sees,
She throws it to the ground and watches it shatter.

She can't run away from this life,
She tires and she tries
But she stops and she stares
At the people who are only living lies.

What made her this way?
She keeps it inside,
A secret that's kept,
Away from the world she'll hide.

She starves for attention,
For beauty and love.
She looks upward at Heaven
And cries to God up above.

What made me this way?
I can't keep it inside,
This secret I keep,
From the world which it hides

Lord change my ways

She flushes her day away,
A day full of pain.
Happiness, attention, and love
Is the only thing she wants to gain.

Discovering the Monster Within

By Patricia Burkley

As I think back, two dates stick in my heart: May 27, 1940 and January 25, 2001. *Why?*

I was born on May 27, 1940, and I would soon learn that I was not a planned child and was definitely the wrong sex. To add more pain to my arrival, my parents were told that they would never have another child because of the physical harm my birth had done to my mom. I was the third girl born to a father who was desperate for a boy. Thus, the stage was set for my development of a low self-worth. When I was six years old, my mom gave birth to my brother, but the negative feelings of those first six years had already influenced my young mind.

As time passed, I felt I had to prove my self-worth. I decided to do my best at everything I tackled. Finally, on January 25, 2001, at the age of sixty, I entered Remuda Ranch in Wickenburg, Arizona – a treatment facility for people with eating disorders. **It was a decision I had made to save my life;** I did, after all, have self-worth.

My childhood was filled with violence, anger, and verbal and sexual abuse. We were poor, but none of us realized that until we were older and had moved to a school district in an affluent town. I had few social skills and little social life around the school. When I joined a church I got involved with the youth groups. While I was elected president of several groups and did my job, I felt I was never accepted as an equal.

The abusive atmosphere at home drove me to study and work hard, and to try my best to succeed at everything I was involved in, so someday I could be free of the dysfunctional madness at home. I was happiest when I was studying, working, and saving. As I got close to high school graduation, I began talking about nursing school. As graduation approached, my father made it clear that there would be no financial help from him as educating a girl was a waste of good money. He said that all women who get educated end up staying at home to make babies!

My mom, however, agreed to help me, and I entered nursing school in September 1958. My usual pattern followed; I was respected and voted into class office, but I had no social life. God did bless me, however, with one special friend whom I have cherished over all the years. She was very brilliant, became my roommate in our second year, and helped me learn how to really study. I joined the choir in my second year and was told that

I could not carry a tune, but if I stood next to someone with a strong voice, I could join.

As a perk for entering nurses training, I was given a complete medical exam. I was placed on a low fat diet because of acne and went through many old fashioned treatments that made my face ruddy after the treatments. The diet made me hungry all the time, and it was then that a monster behavior began ever so quietly – eat a large amount and vomit. It only happened occasionally.

Our school social life consisted of getting together with fraternities from local colleges where it seemed that every male turned into an octopus. This was terrifying to me, especially because of my childhood experiences.

In my senior year, God must have taken pity on me, as I met the man I would spend the rest of my life loving. It was a blind date, nothing fancy; he took me to a hockey game, for hamburgers after (oh no my special diet!) and then hours of talk. He was a gentleman right from the beginning. He showed me (can you imagine – me?) respect. I saw Art as a slim man, and in my head, I decided that I must remain small also. I would not make him ashamed of me.

My senior year was a whirlwind of activity – split shifts of working, dating, and study. What a joy! Art's parents and family accepted me with open arms. Lo and behold, there was friction with my parents, but I was too happy to think it made a difference. His family background was much different from mine – middle class, sheltered, educated, white collar.

On November 18, 1961, I became Mrs. Arthur Burkley. We got a small apartment, I got a nursing job, and our life together began.

After about two years, we decided to begin a family. My first pregnancy, however, ended in a miscarriage, and I was unable to get pregnant again. The doctor told me that I must choose between motherhood and a career. Was my father right? I chose motherhood and quit work.

Carolyn was born, May 14, 1965, followed by David on August 2, 1967. David was a premature baby and needed to stay in the hospital for a week, and I felt it was my fault.

As each pregnancy progressed, I began to eat only what was necessary for the baby, restricting myself to as few calories as possible. I was terrified of gaining weight. The fear of weight gain was fed by images in the media (thin models, actresses etc.), my mother-in-law's disgust with overweight people, and my flawed thinking that I was too big for Art.

When David was one year old, and Carolyn three, I had another miscarriage. One year later, I became pregnant and carried that baby for six months. I had to have an emergency c-section, but the baby died twenty-three hours later. I never saw him or held him.

I was told not to get pregnant again, but I was determined to have another child and got pregnant again in 1970. That pregnancy was difficult, and I was in and out of the hospital the last two months. On February 25, 1971, my son Calvin was born by c-section and my tubes were tied.

The next ten years were busy, and my eating disorder became my constant companion. I was proud of losing weight. I was proud that I could go without eating by ignoring hunger. I secretly vomited when the occasion was convenient. Little did I realize my family and friends knew but did not know how to help me.

I took refresher courses and went back into the work force in 1980. By this time, I had grown into a super-mom, trying to do everything, to please everyone, to fix everyone, and I was running myself down by living on fumes. We had some difficult times, Art and I. My behavior was making him frightened, angry, and depressed. I worked and worked, thinking that if I earned more money, he would be happy. It never occurred to me that maybe I was the problem.

Christmas 1996 was the last day I would see our daughter Carolyn. On June 7, 1997, she called and cut off all communication with Art and me. She said that she had repressed memory about abuse, and that I was a controlling person she had to break away from. My heart stopped. The next two years were devastating, painful, and unreal. She remains estranged to this day.

Art and I were dying inside. I had gone to counseling and he had gone to counseling, but nothing was working. Art had taken early retirement for health reasons. We were both depressed, and needed to get out of the Ohio cold and try to start over.

We moved to Las Vegas in 1998. God planted us in a wonderful neighborhood and opened up the doors to a marvelous church, and we were having a ball. I got a part time job; we traveled, and had family and friends visit. Good life? Yes, but the monster was devouring me.

I tried counseling, a nutritionist, and even called Remuda Ranch to get an estimate of the cost for treatment. I then called our insurance carrier but they denied coverage. My feelings of worthlessness would not let me mention this to Art because I believed I was not worth the cost of treatment.

God, however, had planted a dear friend in my life. She challenged me for months about my irrational thought processes and told me that I was just making excuses. It was really tough love. I got on my knees and asked God to humble me and open my heart to His will.

When I went to Art to ask if I could seek treatment at Remuda Ranch, he had tears of joy in his eyes that I wanted to get well. I have since learned that until a victim of an eating disorder wants to get better, no one can help.

I spent two months at the treatment center for comprehensive treatment of my eating disorder. My journey since then has been mostly upbeat, but punctuated by some down times. God opened up a support team of physicians, counselors, and other health professionals for me. I returned to work because I really enjoy nursing. My team continued to help me until we moved back to Ohio in 2004.

The damage that forty years of the eating disorder had done to my body is devastating. The damage is so extensive, one entire chapter in my book, *Discovering the Monster Within*, which talks about my struggle with eating disorders, is dedicated to detailing the effects on my body. It is a miracle I am alive. God has truly blessed me.

I have been blessed with four grandchildren, and in spite of health issues, I feel that God loves me and wants me to follow and listen to Him. As long as I leave Him in charge and do not take control, life is good.

My desire now is to reach out to others to raise awareness, teach, encourage, and alert everyone to the signs, symptoms, dangers, and seriousness of this disease. I have given presentations at several schools and scouting groups in the hope I can help make young people aware of the illness, symptoms, help available etc.

Without the love, support, and respect of my beloved husband and family, I would not be here anymore. Each and every victim of an illness such as this **needs support, encouragement, and love.** I have learned that God does not make mistakes. He created each and every one of us perfect in His eye and gave each one of us different gifts. Our minds and hearts, however, listen to lies and slowly begin to believe them, not God's truth.

My latest journey began September 14, 2006. I had open-heart surgery, followed by a cardiac arrest, another surgery and three lung taps to drain fluid build up. After a twenty-four day hospital stay followed by three months of rehab. I am glad to be alive.

I have learned not to worry, but pray; not to get angry, but pray; not to listen to the media, but pray. I give all my fears and feelings to God and rest in Him. I know He will take care of me.

I have learned my priorities
1. God
2. Husband and family
3. God's work for me.

I pray that I can keep those priorities as I joyfully welcome each and every day.

Patricia Burkley, who is in her sixties and lives in Ohio, graduated from Cleveland Metropolitan General School of Nursing in 1961, where her eating disorder developed into a forty-year obsession. After practicing briefly, she married and left nursing for fourteen years to raise three children. Patricia re-entered nursing, and has been practicing in the psychiatric field since 1990. Finally, aged sixty, she was convinced to enter an eating disorder treatment facility. She collaborated with longtime friend, Dr. Jack Summers, to chronicle her journey to recovery, which resulted in a book entitled *Discovering the Monster Within*. If you want to get in touch with Patricia, feel free to send a message to
ajburkley@aol.com

Poems by Miriam

Let go of the notion that a well-known pattern provides security and safeness. To keep you ground demands a lot of courage, faith and hope – every single day.

Let Go

Clinging on to something saves you
From having to stand with empty hands
But doing so destroys the dream of flying
Let go
And believe in angels
Or not
But live – vivid!

Nothing Is Heavy

The now is being crushed
From a cloud of nothing –
The nothing fades away
The now voided
From tomorrow on is room again for more
Room for life
For me

Accepting oneself the way we are – probably one of the most difficult tasks (not only) for people suffering from eating disorders.

Untitled

is the universe
too narrow
that even
eye-contact
is too close

head and belly
infinitively distant

in between
my body
I?

and in the middle
my body?
I!

Dreams and hope – dare to dream! And make your dreams become true, step by step, but keep the picture of your dreams always alive.

Untitled

With closed eyes
View the rise of hearts
From the inside
The entire spectrum of colour
Warms the soul

Miriam suffered from anorexia. Now that she is recovered, she is enjoying life and the challenges of being a professional scientist. As team leader and editor-in-chief at www.hungrig-online.de, the biggest German website on eating disorders, Miriam is involved every day in supporting and encouraging people struggling with eating disorders.

My struggle towards recovery, into a new life – in spite of relapse.

The Perfect Girl

By Regina Edgar

My name is Regina. I wrote down my story about three years ago, and it was published in *You Are Not Alone, Volume 1*. Since that time, so much has happened in my life, including my journey into relapse and coming to acknowledge and speak of the fact that I was sexually abused and raped. It is my passion to share with you these steps in my journey, and how recovery is definitely not a 'perfect' process, but a journey with both ups and downs.

I never dreamed that I would be where I am today, and yet, I am here. I am alive. And it is because of this continuation of life that I MUST share my story with you. I believe it is a miracle that I am still living and breathing today, because that life was almost taken from me by a deadly eating disorder, self-injury, and years of abuse.

I grew up in a loving family, although there was always a lot of discord and my parents fought a lot. I was always the peacemaker, and I never made it known that their fighting hurt me too. Many hours I would spend upstairs crying to myself – only to wipe away those tears and put on the smile that everyone loved. I was never a fan of conflict, and so I always tried to make everyone happy. I was your typical people-pleaser, an all-A student, top "Godly knowledge," an aspiring violinist, and a perfectionist all the way. I learned at an early age to do everything within my power to make others feel good and be happy, and to push my own feelings aside. I never got angry. I programmed myself not to feel that emotion – or any emotion. From the conflict in my family I learned that emotions only hurt people. I could not handle getting hurt, so I dismissed my emotions, never dealing with them again. My family was very controlling, but only I could control how I felt.

I was always a skinny little girl. I could eat anything and still be stick-thin. I took pride in that thinness for so long. It was my identity. But, around the age of eleven, it took on a whole new meaning for me. I had been hurt by many people and, because of that, I decided never to trust anyone again. It remained that way for most of my teenage years. My thinness became a quest of destruction and my body repulsed me. Perhaps it was fueled by my hitting puberty, for I was afraid to become a woman instead of a little girl. Regardless of what all took place to lead me there, I started down a deadly path of anorexia. I found out that, even when others controlled everything about me, they could not control my weight or what I ate or did not eat. I was in control of that – or at least I thought I was. At first, I would only eat half of my lunch at school and then I would start skipping breakfast. This went on into my teenage years until it got to the point where I weighed less at the age of fourteen than I did when I was eleven years old. I no longer ate breakfast at all. I threw away my lunch at school and would do my best to eat minimally at dinner time. Often, I would chew my food up at the table – only to spit it into my napkin.

I have always been anemic, but during those years I became excessively so. I got dizzy all of the time and blacking out became a daily occurrence. I passed out or fell down several times but I always kept that mechanical smile – the smile telling everyone that I was all right.

It was at this age that my young career started blossoming. My violin playing became even more so the passion of my life. I started playing the music of my ancestors, the Irish, and became the fiddler for a Celtic band. This band was unique in that it was conceived by my high school administrator and his wife. Upon finding out I played the fiddle, this man asked if I would be willing to join them as one of the key-members of the band. He and his wife seemed so nice and I loved music, so I accepted this offer.

I have always been a hard worker, pushing myself beyond normal limits, but this newfound love fueled this determination further. I practiced seven to eight hours a day and loved every minute of it. The band grew; we produced several of our own recordings and started playing concerts on stages around our state. I felt amazing. My dreams were coming true – but the eating disorder was still there. With the added pressures of 'stage appearance' and the other stresses, my starving myself got even worse as I ate even less and less. I felt I needed to be perfect in all aspects and that included looking perfect. To me, I never saw what everyone else did. When I looked into the mirror, I saw nothing but imperfection.

It was around this time that the man who originally got me into the band, started sexually abusing me. I was about fourteen years old. He started holding my hand, holding my body, kissing me, touching me inappropriately, and he threatened me to not tell anyone. I was a very naive girl, and afraid of what would happen if I told someone about what he was doing with me. This went on for years, several times a week. I felt trapped. His wife was an amazing friend to me, but he told me I could not tell her, or anyone else, what he was doing to me. I believe in God, and I felt that everything that this man was doing to me was against what I believed in. I hated myself more than ever because of what I experienced at his hands. I had no one to help me take the burden of such pain; I was very alone.

Now, I remember it clearly. On December 23rd 2001, my self-hatred and stuffed-pain became too much. That evening, I took out a knife and cut my arm three times. I will never know what possessed me to even think of doing that, but I felt a freedom and a release from seeing what I had done. From that moment, I found out that I could release the pain and my perceived imperfection on the inside by making it visible and painful on the outside. And that started my hellish trek into self-injury. My arms became a battlefield of all the pain I could not express emotionally, and day by day I would cut myself and then roll down my sleeve, put on the smile hiding what I felt, and I once again become the 'perfect girl' everyone believed me to be.

After a while of wearing long sleeves all year round, and wincing in pain whenever anyone touched my arms, people started questioning me. So, I started being even more secretive and cut on my legs instead. It was at that time that I struggled to hide the fact that I was eating so little. People would ask me questions about it and I would have to eat – just to show them that I was 'fine.' That is when I found purging. I felt confident in the fact that I could starve myself, but if anyone ever made me eat I could always get rid of the food by vomiting. In a way, it was yet another way to destroy the girl I was, the girl I hated because of what this man was doing to me. In my mind, the destructiveness was vital, for I could not hang on to the pain that encompassed my very core. The deception was a huge part of everything. I no longer was myself – only a mask of who I thought everyone wanted me to be. And deep down, behind those smiles, there was a girl struggling to survive despite her self-hatred, hidden emotions, and imperfections.

My escape from myself came in three forms: starving, bleeding, or with my head peering into a toilet – a far cry from the confidence I portrayed on stage. I felt so fake, but that was all I knew. The real Regina had been lost since early childhood, when she first found out that she would rather hide emotions than feel the pain of life. I numbed myself out and handled so much horror the only way I knew how.

I played that deadly game for years, getting sicker and sicker, and losing more and more of myself. Then after an amazing stage performance at the age of seventeen, my life – as I knew it – came to a sudden halt. I was diagnosed with a deadly childhood cancer, and my days were suddenly filled with doctors' appointments, surgeries, chemotherapy (losing my hair), radiation, sickness, and hospital stays. I thought that I would die, and doctors, family, and friends believed the same. My whole focus shifted to fighting to live, and I believe my faith is the only thing that kept me alive. God held me, protected me, and gave me the grace to be okay with whatever came in the face of the cancer. I grew stronger in Christ, and I was at peace with whatever He brought my way – be it life or death. I knew that God was in control and that He was being glorified through me.

Still, even during that time, the eating disorder plagued me. I lost a lot of weight because of treatments, but the anorexic part of me loved it that way. I was not able to eat because of the sickness, so they hooked IV food up to me. I cried in the hospital, knowing that that food was saving my life during this cancer, but feeling awful because the eating disorder screamed that I 'was not allowed to have any food' and that I would get fat from it – when in reality, I was a sickly waif wasting away.

After a while, miraculously, the cancer went into remission, and I started to get healthier. I felt it a blessing to even be able to eat without getting sick from chemotherapy, and I thought my worries with the eating disorder were over. After all, I had been given a second chance at life – the cancer did not kill me. I was alive!

However, shortly after I went in to remission, the eating disorder picked up exactly where it had left off. I had gained weight as my health returned, and the eating disorder would have none of it. I fell back into the starving and vomiting. But a new element was added – laxatives. I was determined to get rid of any amount of food I ever had to put into my body. So, not only did I throw up after meals, but I would over-dose on laxatives too. Laxatives made me horribly sick and did much damage to my digestive system. This has left harmful effects on my body even to this day.

I turned eighteen in 2004, and that was the year that the abuse took on a heartbreaking level. That spring, even with all of the abuse he was putting me through, that man raped me – over and over again. My heart sank, the cutting got worse, and of course the eating disorder prevailed. As a little girl, I had dreams of being a virgin on my wedding night, but after that spring those dreams were crushed. That man, old enough to be my father, took something very precious from me, and my downward spiral continued.

I graduated from high school as the class valedictorian, and stood among my peers and teachers, skirt hanging loosely from my deteriorating frame; thinking that after moving away from home to go to college I would find a new life and not have so many problems. At least, that is what I hoped.

I moved to college at Cornerstone University in Michigan, and honestly thought I was doing better. I only ate one meal a day but I truly thought that that was 'normal' and 'okay.' I thought I was better. I had gained weight and I was having fun with friends. I thought I was over any destructive behavior that had plagued my past. Even the abuse seemed to be minimal, for the only times he could hurt me were when we played a concert or I was home on vacation.

It was that first year in college that I met Jessica*. God created a miraculous connection between her and me one evening. She shared the story of her struggle with eating disorders and cutting, and I could not believe my ears. I had never heard of anyone struggling with the same issues I did. So, I told her my story (save the abuse part – I still was afraid to reveal that to anyone) and how I was recovering (which I honestly believed I was doing at that time). However, that same semester, I found myself cutting again, starving more, and purging.

That continued into the summer of 2005, when everything got much worse. I had my own apartment and now was able to be even more secretive than before. The cutting got worse, and I barely ate. My break time at work was spent vomiting into the toilet of a dirty public restroom – desperate to get rid of the food that my co-workers had kindly offered. My evenings were spent compulsively exercising and cutting before I went to bed.

Then Jessica called me one evening when I was hurting so badly. I had been throwing up a couple of times each day, and my legs were a bloody mess of scars and cuts. I confided, for the first time, that I was in trouble. I told Jess what was happening and how I wanted to be free from all of it. So, over the phone, we started a plan to help me get better. I started with eating a small amount of food and tried to keep it down. Jessica and I kept in touch, and I was able to eat somewhat normally for a couple of weeks – which was a huge accomplishment for me. I had not eaten that amount of food at one time in years. Afterwards though, I panicked – I had no way to cope because eating disorders were the only way I knew how to deal with life. I plummeted. I started restricting, purging, and cutting even more. I had publicity photos taken for my music, and I felt that I looked hideous in them. I needed my control back.

I left for Cornerstone for my second year, and the eating disorder was worse than ever. Those first few weeks, I ended up losing quite a bit of weight and I kept getting worse. Jessica was there with me all the way. She finally came to a point where she told me that I needed more help than she could give. So, together (with her posing as me on the phone, since I was crying too hard to make myself do it), we called our school counseling office and set up an appointment for me.

I was scared out of my mind, but I went. It turned out to be amazing, and I truly loved my counselor. From there, I was sent to the school nutritionist, only to find out that my blood levels were not where they needed to be. I was in an anabolic stage, which meant that my body has been feeding off itself for a very long time. This scared those around me because no one knew if my body was feeding off vital organs or not. So, Jess helped me again to start eating a little bit each day, and the nutritionist put me on nutritional supplement drinks to help me get out of the anabolic state. I told my roommates what was going on, and they helped as well.

However, with my eating getting better, the cutting and purging only got worse. I was cutting deeper and more frequently – I was even starting to scare myself. I bled through a lot of clothes, and walking was a huge task because of the pain from the cuts covering my legs I tried so hard to disregard.

Soon after that, I was sent to an eating disorder specialist for therapy once a week. Nothing got better. She brought out painful memories that I had long suppressed. It only heightened my desire to destroy myself. I told no one of the abuse, still too scared to say anything. In fact, I blamed myself for all that had happened to me by the hands of that man. I felt it was my fault and that furthered the resolve to keep it secret. Even more than before, I hated how I looked, and started wearing even bigger clothes than the baggy ones I was shrinking out of. I hated my body and wanted no one to see what I looked like. I despised the face I saw in the mirror.

After about two months of trying to eat, I gave up. I could not do it anymore, and the eating disorder fully took over. I stopped eating. I cut myself multiple times a day, as deep as the strength in my arm would press down. I took laxatives throughout the day and vomited whatever I was made to eat. I got so weak that just walking to classes was a burden. I could not even force myself to practice my fiddle. I had lost interest even in the music that gave so much to my life before – and that truly scared me. I slept most of the time; I had almost no energy to do anything else. I took about three naps a day and awoke only when my worried roommates came in to see if I was all right. I isolated myself from everyone, and found myself getting very depressed.

I restricted my food intake to a minimum, and found my heart racing exceptionally fast one morning. I could barely walk to get into the shower, and kept feeling myself 'start to lose it' and about to faint. It was Sunday, December 4, 2005. I confided in my suitemates how I felt, and they told me I needed to get help. We all went and talked to Jessica, and everyone agreed that I needed further help. They called my counselor, but were disappointed when she told them to wait to see my therapist on Wednesday. I was relieved because I was too scared to get more help. My suitemates and Jessica talked to me and asked questions but I do not remember much of what they said. All I do know is that every time I spoke, they told me that I was not making sense. I was not being coherent. The eating disorder had consumed me and there was nothing rational left. All that came out of my mouth was destruction, and I was too blind from the eating disorder to see it. I fought them, because I could not make sense of what they were trying to do to me.

Wednesday, December 7th, came and I shall never forget that day. Jessica went to therapy with me and told my therapist of her concern. By that time I was in another one of my 'starving escapades' and had not eaten much for a couple of days. I was mentally gone, drained. My therapist called around, and with the providence of God, found ONE bed in all of the area that was open in the psychiatric hospitals. We believed it a miracle that God allowed a place to be open when it seemed impossible. They held the bed for me, and I cried. I remember crying in Jessica's arms while my therapist set up all of the details. I was literally in hysterics as she held me there.

"I don't want to go! I am not sick! Please do not do this to me!" I cried. But, Jessica had the grace of God, and gently held me and told me I would be all right. I know it was one of the hardest things she had ever done. Her strength covered me when I was a wreck there in that room.

I had about three hours before I was to be at the hospital's office. Jessica and my suitemates packed up my belongings and helped me get ready to go. There were many tears and worries as they took me to the psych ward. I felt deserted as I was admitted and separated from my friends. I knew they loved me, but I could not understand why I had to be there, and why I could not be with them. I felt alone. I cried for almost three days straight as I was in group after group, had blood taken and checked, had many nurses checking on me, was weighed every day and was not able to see the weight, was forced to eat, and was monitored at all costs. I felt like a prisoner – and I was scared. I was diagnosed with anorexia and self-injury.

Over the days spent there, I realized that I was not alone. God was with me – even there in a locked up hospital, God was there. And, gradually I started to feel – I mean really FEEL. It was scary. I had never experienced that in my entire life. I felt a tiny bit of 'real-ness' as I sat there trying to eat what they told me to. I had hit rock bottom and had no where else to go. It was there in a psychiatric ward that I hit a breaking point and was able to think clearly for the first time in a long while. I realized that God wanted me to get better. There was more to life out there.

God had saved me by putting me in that hospital. I know that I would have come closer to death over Christmas break if God had not put those people in my life at that time to get me to that hospital. It was there that I realized, for the first time, a little part of me wanted to be FREE for MYSELF. **I, Regina, wanted to get better for me.** I believed that God had a plan in all of this, and I believed that He would be glorified through me. I realized that it was His strength that had given me life thus far, and only His strength could continue to help me out of this pit.

Every evening I would sit at the pay phone in the ward, and talk to Jessica. We talked of God, of freedom, of a better life, of my future – eating disorder-free. I was filled with new ambition and a determination to get better.

I was released from the hospital at a stable weight. I felt that I had a whole new world opened up to me, things would be fine, and I went home for Christmas. Although I followed my meal plan during the Christmas holiday, it was a huge struggle. I cried, fought self-injury, called my friends and journalled often. In one of these journal entries, I remember being very angry and writing down everyone I was angry at and needed to forgive. I was scribbling at a fast-pace when all of the sudden I stopped – I had just written about that man, and right after his name I had written, "for RAPING me." I stared at those words. I had never said, written, nor acknowledged them before. I was taken back; immediately I thought I should erase them or scribble them out. I felt I needed to destroy those words, for he had told me never to tell or write about it *EVER*. But, I could not make myself do it, so I set down my pen, closed the journal, and set it aside. It would be over a month later before I touched that subject again.

I went back to university, started classes, and also started restricting food and cutting again. One night, after I had been exceptionally anxious and cutting a lot, my friends got worried and an emergency call was sent out to the Director of Counseling Services (from the campus) by my RD (who also had been contacted). Those two people, along with my friends, worked to calm me down and keep me safe for the rest of the night. From then on, I was to meet with the aforementioned director every day for crisis stabilization. She became my counselor from that time forward.

Around the 22nd of January 2006, I found myself at an online message board I had been a part of for a while. It was a board devoted to recovery from eating disorders and self-injury, but also recovery from abuse. It was this last category that I was most interested in at that time. I had to know. So, I posted a long entry about my experience with that man, and I asked the board if it was what I thought it was – rape. From there, I ended up showing the same writing to Jessica and to my counselor. It was unanimously confirming – I was sexually abused and raped.

From there, I went into further crisis counseling, and delved into abuse recovery. It all made sense now – the flashbacks, the horrible nightmares at night, my fear of men, etc. I ended the abuse after that – telling him that I told people, screening my phone calls and e-mails from him, watching out and making sure he never came near me again. He ended up lying to everyone, telling them that it was not abuse, but that it was an 'affair.' Most people did not believe him, but, sadly, his wife did. That hurt, as I was once extremely close to her, and that feeling was shattered because of what he did.

With all of the new drama, my eating disorder and cutting continued to get worse. I was sent to the hospital again, but was sent away after one day because my insurance would not pay for it. The hospital tried to get me to eat before I left, but even though I tried, I could not do it. They told me to go straight to the Emergency Room to get fluids and IVs, and I think they all were praying I would not die before I arrived. I was sent back to school, then back home. I continued to get worse. My counselor and I were frantically calling and writing various places to see where I could get help. My insurance would not pay for residential treatment, even though we all knew I needed some long-term help.

I went back to university subject to a strict watch by doctors, nutritionists, counselors, staff, etc. – sometimes even twenty-four-hour watch. Time passed, it became summer, and I still did not have the help I needed. I went to live with a friend in Indiana, and my counselor and I set up a plan to try to gradually raise my food intake. Slowly, by the end of the summer, I was three-quarters of the way towards eating a normal meal-plan. But my metabolism had completely shut down and was no longer working at all, it seemed.

I went back to university in the fall, continued doing all right for a while, and then plummeted. The abuse and all of its ugly memories became too much. I relapsed – *HARD*. Over the next six months, my eating became less and less, and my health deteriorated faster than it had before. My heart started giving out again, I would wake up gasping for breath, and I would go to bed *praying* that I would be alive the next morning. I could no longer walk to classes anymore. I would have to stop three or four times when I walked up stairs. Whenever I did walk (from a car to a building or down the hall a bit), my friends had to slow their steps because I could not keep up.

It was around this time that I had started a new element in my eating disorder: I started restricting liquids. I drank very little, and my body went into a dehydrated, orthostatic state. I was dizzy all of the time, and I blacked out several times a day. My electrolytes were bad again, and I was literally dying. I thought that was the last time I would go through the eating disorder, because I was sure that I was going to die from it. I could not get the help I needed, and I could not get myself out of the struggle.

Towards the end of that year, my body gave up on me. I started losing weight so rapidly that by the time I returned from Christmas break, some of my friends did not recognize me and others wore fearful expressions on their faces. My counselor even looked afraid. I thought I was going to die – it had gone too far; I was not going to make it.

I had an EKG done at an Urgent Care facility because I was feeling so close to death. They did it five different times and could not get a normal/stable reading. My heart was in shock. Again, we tried to get me into the inpatient hospital, but the hospital sent me away after I refused to take medication (medications had caused some serious problems for me earlier, and at that point, I just needed some place to help get my body stable with nutrition – not have people throw pills at me). I was sent back with a 'good luck' and grim faces from the hospital. The thought was, "*This child is not going to make it.*" And, I believed that. However, my counselor did **not** hold that same belief. She held on to **hope** when I gave it up completely. She promised me a life of freedom some day, and she and I kept looking for a place to help me.

Mid-January in 2007, shortly after my twenty-first birthday, I was sent miles away to an eating disorder program near Chicago. I was scared and skeptical, because nothing had worked so far, and I did not think anything or anyone could help me get to a healthier life. However, it was my last hope. I went with all of this in mind. Those next weeks were spent crying, being scared, and feeling very lonely. I made telephone calls to my friends and counselor telling them that I was losing hope; that I did not think I could go on. I struggled through the meal plan they had me on, and my labs and heart-tests were starting to become less dangerous. The whole time I was there, my body continued to be orthostatic and they put me on a regular patterned consumption of special vitamin and mineral drinks.

That was my hardest hospital stay ever, and it was the hardest fight my eating disorder gave me while I was there. The bathrooms were locked after meal times, but as soon as they were open, I was in there purging what I could of what they had made me eat. Also, I was so desperate to 'punish' myself for eating and to numb out emotions, that I would sneak plastic knives from the cafeteria and paperclips from the group rooms in order to cut myself with later.

Eventually, I was able to tell staff about my behaviors, and I was put on "twenty-four-hour watch" (basically, I could not be in a room alone, nor could I go to the bathroom without someone standing in the doorway with their back towards me, making me talk to them the entire time I was using the toilet). I got increasingly angry with people watching me all of the time, and eventually stopped telling them how I was, refusing to trust them. Sadly, this lasted for the rest of the time I was there, although I did start opening up to my inpatient therapist a bit. The program was good for me, though, as I started expressing emotions creatively through art therapy, and I was seeing more and more about myself and this disorder. I felt that this was the first place where I started making significant progress.

After sixteen days, my insurance ran out and would not pay for me to be there anymore. So, with frustration and sad eyes, my inpatient therapist discharged me. I remember her walking me out to my car, giving me snacks to take for the long drive, hugging me, and telling me that I was going to "make it." I did not believe her, and I left there sobbing. Just when I thought I was finally getting some help, I had to be sent back out into the cruel world again. I cried for most of the four-hour drive home. I did not eat, and the destructive cycle was already starting again.

I do not know how to really explain what happened next, except to say that it is definitely from God. After a few days of struggling, I got a determination to fight. I had no more inpatient insurance days left for help, so I figured that if I were to get better I was going to have to do it myself. I started back on my meal plan, my counselor kept me accountable and saw me multiple times a week (plus taking many late-night phone calls), and my friends stuck with me.

I cried. **It was hard.** I gave up a few times, but always got back up (most of the time with other people's help, but sometimes just on my own with God). I successfully gained back the weight that I needed to – my heart gained its health, and my labs increased. For the first time in a long time, I could walk across campus. My friends had to continue walking slower for me as we waited for me to regain my strength, but I could do it! Also, I could climb the stairs up to my room – with no stopping! THAT was such a blessing! **I could** *move* **again!**

In March 2007, with much consideration, prayers, tears, and questions, I decided to make the leap and start the prosecution process towards my abuser/rapist. My decision was not based on what others thought or wanted, but because I want to be a voice to all of those girls out there. By standing up and saying "This is not right! This is NOT acceptable!" I hope to give girls the courage to be able to break their own silence and get out of the abuse that may be happening in their lives even as we speak.

And that is where I am today – healthy and excited to live the life that I always wanted. I feel such HOPE. Whoever is reading this, I desired to write my story and my relapse out for you to reveal the very title of this book, to show you that **YOU ARE NOT ALONE!** Whether you struggle yourself, know someone who does, or even if you are in relapse, the truth is the same – you are not alone. Likewise, I want to let you know that **recovery is POSSIBLE!** Even after ten years of struggling, I found recovery. Yes, relapse may happen, but do not let that discourage you! Keep fighting! There is so much to live for. So much to live for!

Regina Edgar is twenty-three years old and lives in Michigan. She is recovered from a ten-year battle with anorexia. She also recovered from a six-year struggle with self-injury and is a sexual abuse and rape survivor. Regina is a co-writer for *One Life*, a website dedicated to recovery from eating disorders and self-injury (www.river-tree.net/onelife/). If you want to get in touch with Regina, feel free to send her an email at youngfiddler@hotmail.com.

*You can read Jessica's full recovery story in *You Are Not Alone – Volume 1.*

I wrote this poem in the ER (emergency room). I was going through a very difficult time and it was an outlet for me at the time. It really shows the truth of how precious and short life really is.

Your Life's Destiny Is Up To You

By Jana R. L.

It is one day at a time, that is all you have got.
Do not take any moment for granted.
It may be all you get or all you have got left.
Hold the time in your hand like a gift.
Unwrap it slowly and cherish each moment.

Although some days may be hard,
Never hesitate to look to the brighter days ahead.
Make the most of what life gives you.
Learn from the bad times, and cherish the good times.
Always give to others, because you never know when you

Might need that helping hand.
Think of each day as your last.
Would you have fulfilled your purpose God put you on earth to
Do?
Or would you have wasted time with needless things and things
Of society?
Because you see when you die, will you be happy with what you
Did with your life?
Or will you be regretting at how you took so much time for
Granted?
Life is a gift meant to be cherished with all sorts of times you
Have.
What you do with it can only be determined by you.

Jana R. L. is in her twenties and lives in Alabama. She is a singer, songwriter and poetry author. She writes about eating disorders as well as many other things she has gone through. Jana has struggled with anorexia and bulimia for many years now, but still sees the light in getting better. "I believe my faith and hope has kept me going this far. I hope my writings can touch and inspire you to see the light through it all!" If you want to get in touch with Jana, feel free to send a message to wjana@bellsouth.net

A Hunger for Acceptance

By Whitney Greenwood

It is difficult to know where to begin with the story of my struggle with eating disorders, so I will start at the beginning.

I began suffering from low self-esteem at a very young age. I was diagnosed with Attention Deficit Hyperactivity Disorder (ADHD) at the age of one and a half, because I had it so badly. I hardly slept until the age of three when I was placed on medication. Other people did not understand ADHD, and I discerned when I was very young that there were people who thought that I was simply a bad child. This made me even more frustrated, and I often acted out my frustration with tantrums and sulking. Of course this did not make me feel any better because it led me to believe that I must be a bad little girl.

School

I was placed in Head Start preschool at the age of three and again at the age of four. This helped me learn better social skills before I entered Kindergarten at the age of five.

I began first grade in a school that did not teach phonics, and I could not learn how to read using the memorization method. I felt that I just could not read, as did the school who told my mother to send me to Catholic Family Services. So, my mother began to teach me to read on her own, and I later moved to another school which taught phonics and within three weeks I became the top reader. Yet I often felt as if I was not smart enough, even though my teacher said I was.

When I was in third grade I was in a very noisy classroom and had great difficulty concentrating and was falling behind in certain areas such as Mathematics. This convinced me I was stupid. On top of that, some of my classmates made fun of my religion, which was hurtful. Racial prejudice directed at my being of mixed race by adults I met in public further lowered my self-esteem.

Home School

Later that year – I was eight years old – my mother began home schooling me after speaking with a former public and private school teacher, who helps home-schoolers. My test scores quickly improved, and I soon improved by two grades in Math.

Weight Worries

Around this time I began worrying about my weight. In my eyes, I was fat and stupid, and I also began suffering from depression and anxiety, which is common with ADHD sufferers. At the age of ten I made my first attempt at dieting, throwing my breakfast away, refusing to eat certain food, and the like. This only lasted about a week since my mother obviously suspected what I was doing.

Bulimia Nervosa Develops

At the age of eleven, I made the decision to purge. From a young age I was a nervous eater and always ate when I was upset or excited. My mother told me that if I did not get my eating habits under control I would get fat when I got older. My response came at one picnic at a friend's house. After eating a large amount of food, including desserts, I stole into the house and into the bathroom where I made my first failed attempt at purging. I was determined to try again. The problem continued, and my purging slowly increased over time. At the same time I also began abusing laxatives and diuretics when I binged and also began going on fasts.

Inferiority Complex

A big contributor to all of this was that I never felt good enough and did not like my personality. I thought that I had to change the way I was for most of the people around me. I was very susceptible to believing anything negative someone said about me. My mother and I were also victims of emotional abuse.

When I was in my early teens, I was determined to lose weight at all costs. Even though my friends told me that I was thin, I still felt fat and ugly. I was purging more often at this time as well as binge eating and fasting. I hated it when others made me eat when I was in the middle of a fast or when I gave in and ate large amounts in private because I was so hungry after not eating.

An Attempt at Recovery

When I was nearly fourteen, my mother caught me purging, and my step-father threatened to put me in a hospital. Later I learned that this was an empty threat, as he did not know what to do. They told me that I had to get better, and my mother spoke to the husband of a friend who had helped a woman with bulimia. I really did try to get better, mainly to please my parents, as I was so controlled after meals as well as being controlled as to when and how much I ate. Being controlled by others only makes eating disorder sufferers worse, as the eating disorder is way of getting back some of that control – a method to feel in control when one has relatives who always seem to make the eating disordered individual's feelings invalid, and override their decisions.

Bulimia Non-Purging Type

I did cut back on purging, going weeks, even months at a time without doing so. But I still would purge when I binged, in addition to making many strict diet attempts. I did not know at that time, that there is a subtype of bulimia, known as bulimia non-purging type, which is mainly what I suffered from for the next year and a half. In simple terms, this eating disorder is overeating followed by fasting. It usually goes unnoticed by others (as does bulimia purging type) because sufferers are often close to normal weight.

Heading Towards Anorexia Nervosa

When I was almost sixteen, I gradually but quickly began cutting more and more foods out of my diet and eating less and less until I was severely starving myself. I wanted to feel powerful and to show that I could do it. Others were not strong like me; could they starve themselves and exercise on top of it? Of course not, so I gained a false sense of esteem. Yet, I could not get thin enough; even when my friends began telling me that I was losing too much weight, I wanted to lose more. My stomach was not flat enough, my waist was not small enough, I felt too heavy, and worst of all I would demonstrate a weakness with food if I gave in! Whenever I exceeded my quota I purged.

In spite of the fact that I earned straight As in high school, was at the end of twelfth grade level in language arts at the end of eight grade, and had a college level vocabulary at tenth grade, I only felt smart enough when I felt thin enough.

I had been suicidal since I was around nine years old, but it was getting much worse. My relatives were always finding fault with my mother and me and treated me as if I was a complete pain to be around. I often felt left out by many of the teenagers I knew, and I felt as if others would be better off without me.

At the age of sixteen, I attempted suicide and ended up in the emergency room. The hospital would not allow me to go home until I signed a paper promising not to hurt myself and list anyone I would call if

I felt like harming myself. I also had to speak with a mental health professional who said it was safe to send me home.

After my heart had been monitored and my blood had been tested and I had spoken to the mental health counselor, I was prescribed an antidepressant by the emergency room doctor, given a card for a counseling center and sent home. Had they known that I was starving myself, they may not have released me.

This was a very traumatic and humiliating experience that I did not wish to repeat. All I really wanted was to be loved and accepted; yes I had a hunger for acceptance.

Recovery

I entered counseling with a clinical social worker who specialized in treating eating disorders in September 2003. At first I did not want to go; I was only going because my parents and my physician said that I had to. To be honest, I really did not want to get better. Then even when I did, I wanted to put it off until I had reached my weight and food restriction goals so when I recovered I could say that I had accomplished that. I had not yet reached the point where I met all of the criteria necessary to be diagnosed as suffering anorexia nervosa, so I fell into the 'eating disorder not otherwise specified' (EDNOS) category, and, due to my history, bulimia nervosa. It may sound strange, but I wanted to be diagnosed as being anorexic, and I am positive that if I had not received help when I did, I would have eventually succeeded.

When I started working on recovering, I started with trying to eat healthier and later began working on not purging as often. Later, when my counselor retired, I went to another equally good counselor.

Even when I was really working on not purging I did have lapses at times. I remember when I was seeing my second therapist I berated myself because I had gone nearly three weeks without purging and had to start all over again. I had to learn that this was normal, and I was making progress faster than some others. By October 2005 I had gone an entire year without purging, but then I had a lapse and it happened twice. This time, however, I was determined to learn from it and use it to my advantage. In February 2006, I again lapsed several times from the stress of college. I am happy to say that it has not happened since, and I do not believe it ever will again. Even if it did, I am determined to fight back.

How I Recovered

In order to recover, I had to learn how to deal with stress without stuffing my feelings with food or starving my anger. I had to learn that no matter how overbearing my mother's relatives could be, or how many other teenagers hurt me, or how lonely and left out I felt, I was in control of something besides my weight. I learnt that I did not have to be perfect at everything (something I am still working on), and that I was not ugly and did not need cosmetic surgery on my face. These are not things that can be overcome overnight, just as an eating disorder can take anywhere from several months to several years to overcome.

I also had to unlearn food and weight prejudices I had carried for such a long time. It took me two years to get to where I was eating normally most of the time without dieting or compulsively eating followed by excessive dieting. It took me three and a half years to totally give up my black and white thinking concerning food.

Support groups such as Overeaters Anonymous, and especially Eating Disorders Anonymous, really helped me in seeing that I was not alone in this struggle, and I have to say that some of the twelve steps, in addition to the eight steps of the organization, Anorexia Nervosa and Associated Disorders (ANAD), have proved very useful at times.

Journal writing and the homework assignments in books such as *Bulimia – A Guide to Recovery* and *Anorexia Nervosa – A Guide to Recovery* were instrumental in my fight. Prayer, Bible study, and spiritual activities have been vital. The anti-depressant/anti-anxiety medication my physician prescribed also helped quite a bit.

Another great help was the assurance from my friends that they still loved me and believed in me and did not think that I was less of a person. I say to all of you friends and family members of eating disorder victims, please be patient and supportive.

Conclusion

I have learnt that I am a worthy person, and I do not have to be the most beautiful woman in the world. Yes, I still am working on my low self-esteem and not worrying so much about my weight, if someone is prettier than I am, or about whether or not other people think that I am annoying and stupid. On occasion I overeat or under-eat when under stress, but for the most part I eat a healthy and balanced diet. I did it and you can do it too. *DON'T EVER GIVE UP. You are not alone.*

Whitney Greenwood is a twenty-one year old, multi-racial (minorities get eating disorders too), student from the United States. She recovered from bulimia, anorexia, occasional self-injury, and suicidal tendencies. She also struggled with Attention Deficit Hyperactivity Disorder, and is in recovery from a mood disorder and anxiety.

Poems by Tricia L. Fowler

A 'New Hope' was written for a therapist I had at the time. To no avail, she tried to get me out of my eating disorder. Unfortunately, I was so heavily in my eating disorder that I identified myself as my disorder. However, she was able to help me give up the self-harm behaviors that I was doing to myself. She was leaving, and it was my way of saying "Thank you and good bye."

A New Hope

Treading quietly through the shadows of darkness, she knows there is something missing, there has to be more. She sees a glimmering light ahead. Could this be what she is looking for?

Slowly, she moves toward it but stops because she is unsure about what lies ahead, uncertain about herself and, especially, of others. Would it be like before? Her self-portrait destroyed by people she once trusted and believed in? They had lied to her and made her feel unworthy of everything good. They demolished her faith by their mocking and false accusations.

If she continues toward the light, she wonders, would her life become better or is it another mirage that will cast her back into the depths of darkness? Although she lives her life in darkness, it is what she knows, what she is comfortable with. Any other way seems hopeless, unattainable, and would be completely out of her norm.

Yet the light seems so warm, it feels so right, and she just cannot restrain her curiosity. As she takes additional steps, she gently, cautiously, moves toward it. She sees the light is getting brighter, and the warmth is most pleasing to her whole self.

She is willing to take the risk of failure again, and she knows she may find herself back in the darkness, but now she knows that even though she is there that eventually a light will glow once again. She will be the one to make that choice; no demon large or small can take that from her.

The light radiates an inner strength she never had before. She has the strength to overcome horrid pasts, ugly memories, and anything that has frightened her in the past. She has a stronger ability to cope with things that once overwhelmed her. She realizes that there are still demons out there but her being aware of their existence gives her the power to fight them. She also knows that sometimes some things are too tough to handle alone.

Circle of Friends was written for a group of loving and caring people who help each other with our daily ups and downs. We help each other make it through the bad days and celebrate the good ones.

Circle of Friends

A never-ending circle that continues to grow
All across the world to everyone we know
A band of friends all across the globe
Is worth more than all the weight of gold
Our strength in numbers increase every day
Praying for each other all along the way
This band cannot be broken, its strength relies on us
Helping one another, sharing each other's trust
When we have a bad day and everything is a mess
That is when the rest of us are at our very best
Knowing one another, we all understand
We all from time to time need a helping hand
We really need each other every waking hour
With our love and patience we have a special power
The night might get lonely and fears may arise
Just look in the mirror and see us in your eyes
We all are there for you till the morning's dawn
A new day before you helps you carry on
So put your faith in the Lord above
He will send us all his everlasting love

Tricia Fowler is in recovery from anorexia and bulimia. If you want to get in touch with Tricia, feel free to send an email to giraffe_lover_forever@hotmail.com

"I would like to be able to help others as I have been helped. I have struggled with eating disorders for about twenty-seven years, and I am finally at a place that I am proud to be. I am on the road to one hundred-percent recovery and I would not be where I am if it were not for the support of two very special people. Patti was there to support me and helped me find Viola Fodor (www.violafodor.com). Viola guided me through a life process in which I have learned to love myself just the way I am. I am beginning to experience what life is truly about. I take one day at a time, and I am enjoying life. Now, **I am living** *not just existing*. I am currently working on a book, *The Issues Behind The Disorder*, which begins with my earliest memories of my life to where I am today. Feel free to contact me – I would like to be able to help others as I have been helped."

Singing My Truth

By Robin Richardson

I want to begin my story with a song that came through me like a bolt of lightning when I was in my late-twenties. This song tells my story and my truth. It became a lifeline that kept me sane and gave me something to hold onto when I thought I was simply crazy and a bad person. It held the secrets of my past and the reasons why I had become so obsessive and self-destructive, not just with food but in many areas of my life. I cannot write about having an eating disorder without telling the story of the secrets and shame in my family of origin.

Fiction Is My Family

Mama what you feeling? I just can't see behind your lies.
Daddy's been stealing into baby's room at night.
Married to your Maker but who'll see you through these lonely nights?
Daddy's found a better way to meet the needs you always denied.... you always denied.
'Cause Fiction is my family. Pictures don't tell half the story.
Smiles that lie but eyes can't hide the pain. No, not this pain.
Brother's gone crazy, too much blame for one small heart.
Sister up and moved away, distance was her best escape.
Mama stop your preaching, got God and the Good Book on your side.
Turn the other cheek, she told me, it'll be alright, be alright.
'Cause, Fiction is my family. Pictures don't tell half the story.
Smiles that lie but eyes can't hide the pain. No they can't hide my pain.
Mama what you feeling? I just can't see behind your lies.
You just keep on making up the family. I'll just keep on singing my truth.
Gonna sing my truth. Gonna tell the truth.
'Cause everything is gonna be alright. It's gonna be alright.

I am an incest survivor. I am also a recovering bulimic, anorexic, and compulsive overeater, as well as a recovering alcoholic. These are my truths, and yet I am so much more than these labels. For me, recovery means recovering a loving and trusting relationship with myself. It means recovering all the parts of myself I had abandoned and of recovering my place in the world. Today, I am thriving. **I am free** of food and body obsession, free of self-hatred, and free of needing to escape my feelings. Instead, I am able to embrace my life and be who I believe I was intended to be before any of this happened. I am no longer ashamed of myself or my past. I found great relief in telling my most shameful secrets and by holding up to the light all the things that I felt were unacceptable about myself. I used to believe that no one was as damaged, crazy, or incurable as I was and that no one had been molested for as long as I had been. This simply is not true.

There are many people with painful secrets and life stories – and of those, many of them are recovering, happy, and successful today. Incest is not who I am, it is only a part of my story – a part of my past. **I cannot change what happened to me, but I can change the way I view it and the way I feel about myself.** My struggles with self-hatred, food, weight, and voicelessness have made me who I am today. They have given me the gifts of compassion, wisdom, and strength, and a real love of singing and truth-telling.

I hope my story will convey to anyone who is struggling that nothing is too big, too shameful, too dark, or too difficult to be overcome and turned into a source of light and usefulness to others. I love myself and my life today – this seemed impossible when I was living with an eating disorder. I know that my worth is not my weight but rather the love in my heart and the light I shine on the world. Each person who struggles with disordered eating has her own story of pain, her own song of truth, and her own right to tell a new story so that she may transform her life. I am a different person today than the girl and young woman who had no voice and who hated herself, who wanted to disappear by either being so small that no one would notice her, or so large that no one would want to take advantage of her.

My eating disorder had its roots in my early childhood but did not become noticeable until my adolescence. In my family, food was love. It was also a sign of abundance and the only allowed indulgence in a very religious home. My mother took pride in supplying a great variety of baked goods and candies and showed her love by cooking our favorite foods and preparing big Sunday dinners. I was my mother's helper and loved to cook and bake with her, often sneaking extra bites of sweets. I was the youngest of three children and my role was to make everything look good. I did this by being the classic "good girl." I baked cookies, ironed my father's shirts, got A's in school, and went to church.

I came from two generations of Christian Scientists on both my mother's and father's sides. My mother was a faith healer and a teacher of the religion. My family did not drink alcohol or caffeine, smoke cigarettes, take any kind of drugs or medicine, get vaccinated, or even go to the doctor. We never talked about, noticed, or paid any attention to our bodies and my parents turned off all TV commercials that talked about sickness or the body. Sex was only for procreation and never mentioned. The only physical contact I saw between my parents was my dad's off to work peck on my mother's check each morning.

We had a "no talk" rule, never talking about anything but love, peace, and joy. We had no ability to understand or talk about feelings or process conflict. So, when I was sexually molested by family members, I did not tell my parents. This abuse went on from the time I was very young until I was about twelve. After that age, the abuse was emotional and physical, but no longer overtly sexual. I was afraid to tell because I thought it was my fault because I wanted attention. I also was afraid that the abusers would get in terrible trouble. More than anything, I had no way to communicate about or understand such a forbidden subject. Over time, I buried those events in my unconscious. As many young children do, I believed my home and family were perfect, and my parent's God-like.

When I was in the eighth grade my family moved from a bustling community in Michigan to a sleepy little town in Ohio. I went from a private fine arts school to a public school. We moved in the middle of the year, and I was terrified and shaking my first day of school. Worse, all the girls at the new school decided they did not like me. At a party one night they cornered me in a room to confront me with all the things they did not like about me. They did not like the way I acted or talked; they did not want me to have anything to do with their group; and they thought I was conceited.

I was completely shocked, full of shame, and I told no one as I felt I must be bad to be treated in this way. School became unbearable. I decided that I would do whatever it took to be liked, asking these girls how I should be and how I should talk. I became even more pleasing and sweet and gave up my power to the popular crowd. I began asking all the wrong questions, such as, "Am I okay with you?" and "What can I do for you to like me?" I even did the other girls' homework and let them cheat off my paper during tests. I lost myself in order to be liked and became someone I did not know

At the end of eighth grade, I went on my first diet and discovered that I got attention by losing weight. To me, I had found the secret of being liked; if thin was applauded, and then thinner was better. Those same girls that would not speak to me now wanted to know how I lost the weight. I kept losing weight until I was frighteningly thin. Always anxious, I became even more afraid and began pulling out my hair compulsively. During the ninth and tenth grades, I wore a bandana to school each day in order to cover my bald spots. No one in my family, except for my mother, even mentioned my weight, baldness, or eating behaviors.

My mother attempted to help me by praying to relieve my anxiety. We prayed together but without results. It was as though my body was screaming the shame and pain that my mind was not aware of. At the end of the tenth grade, I got too much sexual attention from boys and the eating switch turned to on. I started to eat and could not stop. I gave up pulling out my hair and began to use food to quell my anxiety. I gained many pounds rapidly... then more and more... until my weight nearly doubled from what I used to be. My body size said the "No" and set the boundaries with boys that my voice simply could not speak.

Food was my comfort, my numbing, and my safety. It was my relief from all the things I could not talk about. Yet, I hated being overweight. I was at war with myself, and I hated my body because I thought it had betrayed me. I was on a vicious cycle of dieting, exercising, and bingeing that only masked my self-hatred, shame, and loneliness. I simply could not stop overeating. Food was my best friend, and I turned to it for everything – fun, relief from boredom and stress, a way to bond with others. I took on the role of being everybody's friend and the "fun girl" but secretly longed to be like my thin, beautiful girlfriends. I did not have a boyfriend or date for most of my teenage years until my senior year in college, until I lost weight. I wore skirts every day so that I could hide my fat and my sexuality. I exercised fiercely though, and tried every kind of extreme fad diet and even fasted. Every one of these attempts ended in failure. I would end my diet with a binge and then eat continually until I gained back whatever weight I had lost, plus more. This created only more shame and self-distrust.

I discovered bulimia in my senior year at college, and a whole new struggle began. I felt possessed by a gnawing energy or anxiety that would take me over, and the only way I could deal with it was to throw it up. I threw up the inner tyrant of perfectionism that demanded I be brilliant, successful, and land a great job when I graduated. I threw up my mother's demands that I be the next healer in the family, marry a Christian Scientist, and carry on her work.

I lived a double life, smiling on the outside and dying on the inside. My life was a carbon copy of my mother's life. My senior year of college, I dated a Christian Scientist from MIT (as was my father). I attended Wellesley College (as my mother did) and then worked on Capitol Hill in Washington DC (as she had) after graduating. I then worked at the Christian Science Monitor (her dream for me), the whole time bingeing and purging. My mask of having it all together began to crumble as my days became solely about how to get food and how to get rid of it. Bulimia took over my life and for five years I binged and purged several times a day.

I hit a bottom at the age of twenty-four, when I found myself completely alone, unable to work, throwing up blood, and shaking all the time. I desperately wanted to stop the bingeing and purging – I actually had dreams that I was going to die – but I could not stop. I had to hit a bottom where the pain of bulimia was worse than the pain I was trying to stuff or purge. The faith that I had had as a child evaporated and I became angry and resentful with the idea of God or religion.

My miracle happened when I asked for help. I got into a minor car accident, which led me to run into an old acquaintance, a woman who just two years before had been dying of anorexia. When I met her on this day, she was clearly happy and healthy, and her eyes were sparkling. She talked to me about how she had gotten well and gave me hope that I could get better too. Through her, I found help and a recovery community. I went to therapy and began to talk about my secrets and the pain of the things that had happened to me. I began to recover from bulimia and was able to find my voice as I let go of the shame of being abused. After several years, I was finally able to pursue my own (not my mother's) life's passion – singing and songwriting. I moved to Nashville, found love and a music partner, and began to travel the world performing, truly living a dream.

I wish I could say that I lived happily ever after, but I cannot. Recovery for me has not been a straight line, but a spiral of learning, healing, falling down, and getting back up. I am forty-five years old, and my last bout with anorexia ended almost nine years ago when I got sober from alcohol. I had been performing music for many years in a traveling band, unaware that I was drinking more and eating less.

My bottom with alcohol happened when I was faced with my husband's secret sexual addiction. I realized I had created the same fantasy and blindness that I had in my childhood – that I had a perfect family or perfect marriage. In a moment of truth, I was able to see myself and my alcoholism clearly. This led to another round of surrendering, recovery work, and healing. I found I had a lot more work to do with my family of origin, changing the dynamics with them, and again finding the places I had abandoned myself. I went back to school to get a degree in therapy. My healing spiral of recovery is about gaining self-knowledge, living more and more in my truth, and of loving myself. **My heart became open to life and love again when I was able to truly forgive those who had harmed me.**

Recovery from disordered eating is a journey. It is NOT about being perfect. In fact, it is about learning to be human, developing balance and a calm and loving center. I had a lot of slips at first and learned to view them simply as reminders to show me what needed my attention. Instead of self-criticism, I worked hard to develop compassion for my struggles and learn skills of self-respect. Over time this grew into self-love and self-trust. To recover myself, I had to stay with myself and learn about me; who I am, what I care about, value, and desire most. Instead of blocking out my feelings, I had to learn how to cry and to make space for all my feelings without judging any of them as wrong or bad. Setting boundaries, saying "no," and developing assertiveness were essential skills I had to learn in order to be in relationship without giving myself away. Instead of turning to food for love, comfort and relief, I had to ask for what I needed from safe others. I also learned to nurture and calm myself and to find and fill my deepest hungers in healthy ways.

Today, I do not view my eating disorder as something I hate or even regret. It was how I survived and kept the truth of my childhood from myself until I had the support and strength to deal with it. Because of the early abuse, it was important for me to develop my own spirituality, one that allowed for the horrible things that happen in this world and had happened to me. I created my own "family of choice" or supportive community. This is what I learned: to stop abusing myself, I had to feel the pain of having been abused; to have a voice, I had to give back the shame that silenced me to the ones who had abused me; to stop being a victim, I had to own my power and build relationships that are respectful and supportive; and to heal my sexuality, I had to learn that I truly do matter and that no one ever has the right to touch me sexually if I do not want them to. And, most amazingly, through this healing process, I now have my family back in my life. What a gift!

Through my years of struggle with food and weight, I completely lost touch with whether I was hungry or full. This was a skill I had to develop by constantly practicing listening to my body's subtle cues. I needed to restore my relationship with my body as I had hated, abandoned, and abused it for years. I did this through yoga, dance, hiking, and massage. I learned what foods were healthy for me and what foods actually set up cravings. I had to separate emotional from physical hunger and commit to eating only when I was actually hungry and stopping when full.

My eating disorder served as an early warning system that gave me important information before my conscious mind was even aware there was a problem. If I reached for food when I was not physically hungry, I had to find out what was beneath the craving and then take action to get this need or desire met. I did this by asking myself what it is that I do not want to feel or to know. Then I would write in my journal, talk to a friend, pray, or sing until I became clear about what the real issues were. It is amazing to me that talking or writing about whatever is bothering me – especially the things I am most ashamed of – <u>takes the compulsion away</u>.

At first, recovery used to take up most of my time. I heard the saying "five miles into the woods, five miles back out." I was told that I would need to spend as much time and energy on my recovery as I did in my eating disorder, which was most of my time.

Today I do not spend my time worrying about food or my body. I always remember, however, who I am and where I am coming from. I live with an anxiety disorder, and I am a trauma survivor and a recovering alcoholic and addict. It is important for me that I continue working on a recovery program, have a healthy lifestyle, and get help whenever I need it. The years of struggling with anorexia, bulimia, and compulsive overeating have caused permanent damage to my body – to my digestion, metabolism, thyroid, and reproductive system. Considering all the years I abused myself, **I am grateful to be alive** and as healthy as I am.

As I am human, I still have bouts of perfectionism, shame, negativity, or fear. The difference now, though, is that I can trust myself to treat myself lovingly and make healthy choices despite my feelings or problems. I have many tools for changing the channels of negativity and fear. I am free physically, emotionally, and spiritually and I am living a life beyond my wildest dreams. I know that anyone who is struggling with an eating disorder or a difficult past can find his or her way to freedom also.

Robin Richardson, from Boulder, Colorado, is recovering from anorexia, bulimia, and alcoholism. She is also an incest survivor who is now thriving in her life. A singer-songwriter and inspirational speaker for all age

groups, Robin is also a psychotherapist working with disordered eating, sexual abuse, and addictions. Robin's newest CD, *Wild Bird*, chronicles her journey out of addiction and despair into peace, self-love, and a life worth living. *Wild Bird* is available on www.sunlightofthespirit.com.
For more information about Robin, visit www.robinrichardson.net

Robin's song, *The Angels Came* is featured on the *You Are Not Alone Companion CD.*

Poems by Jennifer

For Craig

You stood alone against my foe
And watched me dying very slow.
You fought in every way you could
And I panicked at your shifting mood.
I promised, begged and asked you to leave
This ugly battle just to me.

I tried to fight this incipient monster
With all the strength that I could muster.
But it had snuck in and grabbed ahold
It wanted my body, it wanted my soul.

The scariest thing to you for certain
Was that I did not see its' determination.
It called me fat, gross and weak
It made it so I could not eat.
And yet, I felt fine
But it had left me blind.
It made it so I could not feel
Its' need to take me and to kill.

You screamed, you yelled with belly burning
Your mind, your thoughts, always churning.
You could not find a place to rest
Left alone in this frightening mess.
You ached to find what once was yours
Yet you feared it was gone for ever more.

At a place of transition
I surrendered, an act of submission.
I went to war, it to match
At a place called Remuda Ranch.
You were left alone at home
Connected only by the phone.

And yet your love and fighting spirit
Gave me strength so I could do it.

Home again and not yet whole,
I let you see my exposed soul.
In hopes that you will begin to feel
That this new beginning is real.
I understand that it will take time
To earn your trust and ease your mind.

I need your love, I need your care
But now this battle I will share.
I now will take the reins
And give you time to rest again.
I know my dear that you are weary
But please understand that I see clearly.
The snake that had tried to eat me whole
Is dying and leaving behind what it stole.

The bite still stings
And sometimes brings
Thoughts and feelings that shouldn't be,
However, now that I have the ointment
You can trust I have control of this assignment.

So rest my dear
And do not fear
Believe that with my will and my skills
Our life again will be filled.

My Gift

It is a gift.
God gave it to house my soul.
And yet it feels as if
It is not mine alone.

It was used by a monster
To satisfy his rage.
It is used by my lover
Because it is what he craves.

I should love this body
Is what they all say
But it is owned by everybody
And it always has to pay.

They say that I should get control
Well, that is what I did.
I did it to save my soul
To disconnect from its' carnal bid.

Now you want me to revive
And feed this used apparel.
But I wonder why
Is it just to keep YOU from peril?

The only way I can embrace,
My body once again
Is to truly understand, this is MY place
And mine alone to tend.

To care for it with love
And understand that its' full measure
Was given from above
As a gift to me alone and to give ME pleasure.

© Jennifer

Alone

Alone, alone I try to be
Relentlessly pursued by the fact of me.
To feel that flesh
To acknowledge the debt
That still has yet to be paid.

I feel the sickness in me rise.
Purge, purge the mind it cries.
There is complicity in my soul,
It will never acknowledge its' role
In the ugliness that mars my core

The ugly fact of truth,
That it was me that was used.
That it was me who let it canker,
My soul, like a prankster.
I pretended it was not so
That my mind was clean and pure.
My soul untouched and sure.

Now I must address it
Acknowledge and give credit.
To my body for its courage.
For it has absorbed the carnage.

Now is time for penance.
I am ready now to chance it.
I will open the door
To whatever it stores.
I will see the truth.
I will clean and push.
I will change the mind,
And take the power that is mine!

This body restored
My mind happily cured.
I will face the future

With boldness and verve.
With the feeling "I am stable"
I will be able
To enjoy this life full,
Free, clear, and whole.

Jennifer is thirty-nine years old and lives in the United States. She began her struggle with an eating disorder at the age of thirteen. In spring of 2007, she was admitted to an in-patient treatment facility (Remuda Ranch) for sixty days. She continues to work at recovery and is hopeful that she will finally put this behind her.

My Story

By Jennifer Friedman

Three of my twenty-five years have been entrenched with diagnosable eating disordered behaviors, emotions, and thoughts. For three years my eating disorder wholly disrupted my life with no regard for my relationships, my education, the least of all, my body. Unfortunately, other psychological problems hid my eating disorder and delayed its diagnosis.

While I never realized it when I was a kid, I associated sneaking food with anxiety, fear, and ultimately reward. Attempts to obtain more food than I was allowed set the stage for an argument. Food served as a delaying tactic, a tranquilizer, a possession; it was rarely fuel. When I was out shopping at the mall with my friends when I was ten or eleven years old, they would want to shop; I would want to eat. It occurs to me now that it did not matter where I was, I always gravitated towards food regardless of my appetite.

Despite my childhood anxieties surrounding food, I did not associate it with my body image. I always thought I had a big stomach, but I would look in the mirror and think that my legs were skinny; it did not concern me either way. School, however, was a bit more trying on my self-image as I was mocked daily by boys and girls. The recurring topic of interest among the boys seemed to be my childhood acne – "pizza face" was a real stinger. Perhaps that is why I was not overly concerned with my body – I was focusing more on my face. My FACE was the source of hatred and ugliness. My FACE needed fixing, not my body.

I started paying slight attention to my body when my breasts, without consulting me, began to prematurely "bloom," and were noticed by the boys. One of the real jerks, one who mocked me mercilessly, once ran around the schoolyard with two basketballs under his shirt screaming, "I'm Jennifer!"

I grew up watching *Beverly Hills 90210* and *Saved by the Bell* and apathetically wondered if that was what I would look like when I "grew up." I started becoming aware of how others looked in comparison to how I saw myself, and I always gravitated toward taller, skinnier girls, narrow girls.

When I was fourteen, I had my first serious bout of depression and self-injury. Several years later I was diagnosed with Borderline Personality Disorder. I entered therapy with every good intention, but after six months,

I thought I was better, and quit. The truth was I DID feel better; the latest depressive episode had ended as naturally as they always did, and I did not want to face the likelihood that the cycle would continue.

In junior high school, I had random episodes of fasting, bingeing, and unsuccessful attempts to purge. I do not think it had much to do with my body, but rather, with doing something completely, uncompromisingly RIGHT. (I was later diagnosed with Attention Deficit Disorder, which clearly, in retrospect, played a role – the ability to carry something out from start to finish was key here). Maybe it was the uncompromising need to be accepted; maybe I was taking back control of my body in some way. Maybe if I could starve the right way, if I could get away without eating a morsel, then I was good, safe, in control. And while I did occasionally weigh myself and felt powerful if the scale went down, it ultimately did not have much to do with my body. It was more about wanting to be seen. If my teachers would notice my hunger, in my mind, I'd succeeded. There would be a sense of urgency around caring for me. There would be affection and warmth.

The older I got, the more I associated food with weight. I remember one day in high school looking in the mirror, naked, and declaring to myself, "I am fat. Wow. I really am fat!" I had ROLLS. I was WIDE. I had big ugly breasts. There was simply no room for argument – I was fat!

In the second semester of my freshman college year I took "involuntary medical leave" and went to a day treatment program for Borderline Personality Disorder. My therapist changed my life with her intuition, warmth, artistic understanding, patience, grace, and her tremendous heart. I felt free; I felt able. I declared psychology as my major and moved into an apartment on campus, eager to implement the skills I had learned in treatment.

Unfortunately, the eating disorder mentality started to creep into my daily living. I had never addressed my issues with food because I had never realized I had had any. There was even an eating disorder group at the day treatment program that I could have gone to if I had wanted, but it was a non-issue. Besides, only skinny people have eating disorders, right? I was not skinny. There was nothing to worry about with me.

But during my first semester back at school, I occasionally started trying to control my eating. I would do it for a week or two, then binge and go back to "normal," overeating all the time. I made friends with a girl who had had an eating disorder in the past but had received treatment. It still, however, bothered her sometimes. She would say, "I am having a bad-body day." Pretty soon she started saying it every day. She later said that she knew I had an eating disorder but felt uncomfortable saying anything.

I started seeing a new therapist, Elizabeth (Beth) Kelly in Tarrytown, NY, who taught me that I was a whole person before the onset of my eating disorder which buried that person for three years, and that I am now just a better version of my former self.

Beth has guided me in forming my identity. She saw me at the peak of my victory over cutting, and there she noted my strength. She remembered that strength and used its evidence to guide me throughout recovering from my eating disorder. She is a tough cookie, Beth... as tough as she is charming, genuine, and witty. I owe her so much.

On another note, Beth's physical appearance was a fixed point of reference for a patient constantly in flux. She is tall, lean, and toned, and I was short, curvy and, aside from my forearms which endure daily piano workouts, shall we say… soft. From my lowest weight to my highest, I compared myself to Beth's fixed figure and felt jealous that she seemed to be able to maintain it so effortlessly. I felt foolish and inferior because I was trying so hard to get what SHE had, and the difference in our bodies was so visible, and how could I POSSIBLY be sick when she was thinner than I am and healthy? I am CLEARLY making a fool of myself here!

Fortunately, I could see past that as she guided me in my recovery, but because I realize it is a common problem in a therapeutic relationship I felt it necessary to discuss here.

Back at school, I was so excited about studying (something VERY uncharacteristic of me!) for my psychology classes that I went a couple weeks eating just a little without noticing, caring, or speaking of it in therapy. After two weeks of intensive studying, I realized I had unintentionally (maybe-somewhat-intentionally) lost some weight and thought, "hey, I should keep this up."

This was when it first became an internal struggle, an entrapment, a quest to consciously defy my hunger, a self-statement of, "Now I HAVE to keep going."

I spent the year documenting everything I ate and berating myself constantly. I would wake up in the morning and think, "How can I control my eating today?" I have a journal filled with this stuff. I made lists of everything I was doing each day and carefully plotted out all my meals. However, as inhibiting as that may seem, it really was just the pre-cursor, the sub-clinical stage in the development of my eating disorder.

I spent a year refraining from cutting and implementing erratic eating patterns at the same incremental rate. As the cutting got better, the eating got worse, and I did not catch on. The following fall, at twenty-two years old, my sub-clinical eating disorder now developed into something tangible.

After a month of starving during the day and bingeing at night, I decided that this time I was going to do it for real – this was when the scale entered the picture, the calorie-counting, the compulsive list-making where my days were divided into fifteen minute increments – and it all revolved around food. I stopped caring about my beloved music classes. I knew that I was doing it... and I felt solace in it.... but I remembered somewhere in the back of my mind that I wanted to be in those seats, in the choral hall, in the classrooms with permanent staff lines on the blackboard. I wanted there to be a portal wherein the enrichment just seeped, and maybe I would be able to take something away from this. But as it was, I just went to class to distract myself from food.

I received a hurtful artistic criticism from a teacher one day and vowed not to eat the rest of the day.

I ate the same thing every day.

I would not eat with people.

I made myself starve all through the night before and the morning of my piano final so I would be able to justify to myself why I failed.

The first time I purged, I felt like a conqueror. Herein lay my new major. It was a few weeks into the restricting, just after bingeing, and I felt I had just entered into something surreal, something that I had never thought I would be able to do. It felt like an ability rather than a weakness. I felt like I won by getting sicker. I felt like I was going to have a real, valid, accountable illness now, and I was glad for that.

I was weak all the time from the restriction and bingeing and purging, I was dizzy and got head-rushes, and my vision got dark and fuzzy. I was scared to go to sleep at night because my heart was palpitating in order to keep my body working. I felt bad for my heart. I was terrified of the heart palpitations and equally terrified to eat in order to stop them. I had to train my mind to dissociate, to visualize my heart as a piece of cardboard in order to have enough peace of mind to sleep.

What seemed like a quest for victory at the time became a violent struggle just to stay afloat, let alone win. You would think that with all the people I had around me, all the luxuries I had, that survival would not be an issue for me. Those fighting for survival do so in the wilderness or on the streets, not a college campus with tons of practical resources (i.e. food, education, a roof over my head, a bed to sleep in) at their disposal. But eating disordered survival is not that practical. And after seven months,

EDNOS (Eating Disorder Not Otherwise Specified) – which for me consisted of restricting for most of the week and bingeing and purging two or three times a week – turned into no-holds-barred bulimia.

The day which marked my submission to bulimia represents a very clear line for me. I remember that day, and I see my days from the start of my eating disorder until then as my pre-bulimia days, as one phase of the eating disorder, and my days thereon in as my bulimia days, as the second phase of my eating disorder. I crossed over at this point. I remember it was during Culture Shock, an outdoor, highlight-of-the-year, weekend-long campus festival with bands and carnival games and a big old beer tent. I ate some carnival food and did not look back.

I had fallen, and I could not pick myself up. What are the words to describe this? "Terrified" is an understatement. "Hopeless". A demoralizing combination of the two, maybe? I hit a dead end. There are no words for it.

I characterize my post-bulimia days as walking in quicksand. I am walking along, when suddenly, with no rhyme nor reason, nature takes over. My malnourished body falls victim to the finely disguised quicksand; I was well on my way, I did not ASK for this! And now I just want to say, "Okay! I am sorry! I should not have been here in the first place! Please make it stop! Please let me out! Let me pull myself up, please!"

Or in eating disorder speak:

"I am hungry. I have to eat now.... where is the food? I do not care about anything but the food. Weight loss? What is that? I tripped into something that has now eaten me whole... I must keep it here, its taken me hostage and I must appease it.... I just want to SURVIVE. I do not care about losing weight. Oh my God please, please just let no one find out...."

Or:

"Please just let me get it all out, PLEASE, I should not have eaten it all but now I just need to GET IT OUT, OH PLEASE, PLEASE, PLEASE, oh my god, I do not think I got it all out.... oh my God oh my God oh my God...."

My life continued this way until a year after I graduated college.

I dropped out of the Music Conservatory.

I spent days acting chipper for all (I actually developed bulimia in accordance with a social life, so I felt genuine happiness when I was with my friends, much the same as my cutting days in junior high) and nights bingeing and purging in places I'm ashamed to think of now.

I wanted people to know.... but I did not want them to know how, when, where.... God no, this was mine. But I wanted help.... I wanted compassion.... but this was mine. I had lost myself at this point. I was an eating disorder. Every thought I had, even in my dreams, everything was food.

For months, my therapist had been urging me to start seeing a nutritionist who specializes in eating disorders. I resisted for a long time, but finally saw Amy Peck*, a nutritionist who also specializes in eating disorders, in Katonah, NY, and, just for the record, she turned out to be a lifeline. She has helped me realize how my life affects my eating disorder and how my eating disorder affects my life, and she has soothed my nerves time and time again in the aftermath of an eating disorder. She writes me "to do" lists and gives me samples of fish oil. She calls protein bars "medicine" to take away the association with bingeing. Every time I see Amy I leave smiling, relieved, happy, and understood.

So, with the help of both Beth and Amy, two people who took me equally as seriously as one another and cared about me and earned my unconditional trust, I tried, slowly, different strategies to improve my symptoms. I tried structuring my weeks. I genuinely tried, but didn't always succeed; once, for example, I took a three-day-long train trip to San Antonio to visit a friend, and I binged and purged on the train.

I graduated in December 2005 and thought that I could put my eating disordered days behind me. But I soon started bingeing and purging in the apartment when my roommate was not home, even sometimes when she was. Then a friend committed suicide and my grandmother died. After two years of using food to deal with life's stressors, of trying to perfect myself and giving up on it altogether, of living by the rules of scales, calories, food availability and toilet bowls, I was about to enter the worst and final period of my eating disorder.

I started skipping work to binge and purge. I had neither seen my psychiatrist nor taken my medication (Prozac) in months. Because I wasn't medicated, I was both severely bulimic and majorly depressed. I was walking around in a haze, not speaking in full sentences, making spelling and grammatical mistakes in my journal entries, forgetting things.... I was scared and hopeless and decided that I needed inpatient treatment. I made all the phone calls to New York State Psychiatric Institute** (NYSPI) at Columbia University in Manhattan, and was finally admitted.

NYSPI, followed by Renfrew's Intensive Outpatient Evening Program, ultimately got me past my eating disorder, and for this I could not be more grateful. I attended meditation groups, yoga, DBT, role-playing, psychotherapy, medication, body image and self-esteem groups.

And since I usually only cry alone, I was forced to actually cry in front of others. It was unbearable; I loved it.

And I had fun there. I did. We went to restaurants to practice eating in public. There were some genuine moments where I felt like I was just going out to lunch with friends. Sometimes I forgot that I was coming from a hospital. These outings, along with my passes to go out and eat meals and spend the day on my own, gave me a glimpse at what I had long forgotten existed – a life outside my eating disorder.

Recovery, for me, has been the gradual rewiring of the brain to react to discomfort differently than it once did; NOT the disappearance of discomfort itself. Recovery does not equal reversal of all history, all personality traits, that made me vulnerable to an eating disorder. These are the questions that I sometimes carry, but still I believe that awareness alone is evidence of recovery.

Recovery, on my own terms, has been the healthy development of a sense of self that has nothing to do with body or food intake, and that has everything to do with the history and personality that made me vulnerable to an eating disorder. Is there a way to go back in time and take only the good from my history? Sculpt the better, stronger half of my personality into a woman who respects and honors her body? No, but indeed there is a woman worth figuring, whose weaker moments may, in retrospect, aid in the fight toward awareness and self-love.

Jennifer Friedman, a New York native and graduate of SUNY Purchase, first discovered her love for music as a little girl sitting at her parents' piano. She overcame an eating disorder to record an album of her original songs, and begin performing them. For more information about Jennifer, visit and www.jennfriedman.com and www.myspace.com/jennfriedman

*For more information about Amy Peck, visit www.amygpeck.com

**For more information about the New York State Psychiatric Institute, visit http://nyspi.org/Kolb/index.htm

Jennifer's song *Skin* is featured on the *You Are Not Alone Companion CD.*

Poems by Erin Brinkle

This is a conversation between ED (eating disorder) and myself.

ED & I

"Hey, Erin, what's up? How's it going?"
"Ed, what are you doing here?"
"Come on, girl, don't be like that, it's me. Remember? Your ol' pal ED."
"ED, I thought we already had this conversation, we're over, it's done."
"Oh, come on, Erin. Yeah, I know, we've had our bad times, but why can't we still hang?"
"You really want to know the truth?"
"Yeah."
"Okay. ED, I think you're stupid, pointless, and dangerous. I hate you. You ruined my life, you stole my joy, and you hurt my friends and family. ED, it's over, we're through. I want you to get out of my life for good, and stay out! I refuse to be controlled by you anymore!"
"Erin, girl, you can't possibly mean that, I know you don't mean it."
"Yes, I do! What part of "no" do you not understand?!"
"Erin, you know I can't accept that."
"Yeah, well, deal with it in therapy; I've had to, no thanks to you!"
"You're welcome."
"That wasn't a compliment."
"Oh, come on, Erin, don't be such a goodie-goodie. Look, just skip one meal, just one, for old times, sake."
"NO! ED, I'm sick and tired of this crap! I'm sick of you, and I'm not gong to put up with you anymore!"
"It's just one meal! Don't you remember that rush we used to have from seeing your ribs sticking out? That rush we felt when you could put on a certain size of jeans? Remember? Huh?"
"THAT'S IT!!! ED, GET OUT! GET OUT AND STAY OUT! YOU DON'T CONTROL ME ANY MORE!"
"But, Erin…!"
"DON'T YOU 'But Erin' ME! GET OUT NOW!"

"Okay, okay! Jeez, no need to shout! But mark my words, Erin, I'm not done with you yet; I'll be back. You won't know when, you won't know how, but I'll be back."

"Bring it on, ED, I'll be ready for you; I'm not going down, not again! Now… GET OUT!!! Don't you make me get out my tommy gun!"

"Oooooh, I'm so scared"

ED walks away.

"Yeah, that's right, just keep on walking! You know better than to mess with me! Don't start nothing, won't be nothing! And if I catch your sorry face around here again, I will use the tommy gun! I'm not afraid of you!"

© Erin Brinkle

Survivor

I do not know what to
Feel anymore;
I am scared, I am confused,
I am frustrated, I am unsure.
I hate feelings things,
Hate not being able to
Take hold of them
And tear them to pieces;
Scatter them into the
Wind,
And see them fly away,
Far away from me.
Leave me alone.
I do not want to talk,
But I do.
I do not understand me,
Myself, my mind,
Anymore.
There are days when
I feel so full,
So glad, so proud, and
Pleased with me.
Then, there are others
When I feel empty,
Sad. Lonely.
Nothing matters,
There is no joy then.
There is no happiness.
Go away.
I cannot feel, do not want to,

Do not want to see
Myself.
There are days that are
Bright, shiny, and sparkly;
They glisten like jewels.
Then, there are days that
Are dim, rusty, and dull;
They are like raging
Storms.
I wan to cry, I do cry,
But sometimes I do not;
I do not want to seem
Weak.
But soon, someone comes.
They speak kind, caring
Words,
Words of love and comfort.
Arms wrap around me,
Hug and hold me tight.
Then I know
I am not as alone as I
Thought.
My spirit becomes revived.
Renewed.
My thoughts carry me
Back;
Back to blind faith,
And the knowing that God is with me,
That He loves me,
And will never
Leave.
He will not change,

Not ever.
I rest in this,
I feel an unknown
Feeling wash over
Me.
What is it?
It is Peace, at last.
Father God, give me
Strength.
It is in You that I
Trust to pull me
Through.
For without You,
I will fade.
I am a survivor
Of anorexia.

Beauty

Beauty.
It is all around us.
It is everything we
Wish for,
Everything we aspire to
Obtain.
Women want it,
Men are attracted to it,
Nature claims it as
Its own.
Beauty.
What makes someone,
Or something,
Beautiful?
Some see it in cloths
Or make-up fashion;
Some see it in art,
The arts, music, paintings.
Others see it in material
Things,
Like cards, jewelry, homes.
But I see it somewhere else;
I see it in a leaf,
A stick,
A rock,
A blade of grass.
I see it in a mouse,
A fish,
A bird.
I see beauty in a flower,
A butterfly,
A snake,
A lizard.
I see it in the trees,
The clouds,
The sky,
The water.
And, just now, I am

Starting to see it
Somewhere else.
Beauty
Is
In ME.
I am beautiful.
Inside
And
Out

Erin Brinkle is nineteen years old and lives in Texas. She is recovering from a two-year battle with anorexia.

Shannon's Story – Key to Life

Unlocking The Door To Hope

By Shannon Cutts

Through the strange foresight of my mother, I just happen to know that my battle with eating disorders began at the age of two. I was the first-born, and I suspect it is for this reason alone that Mom kept a baby journal in which she enthusiastically chronicled my early days (it is worth mentioning that her zeal for preserving minor details, such as how often she changed my diapers, had waned by the time my baby brother came alone – there is no known such sentimental chronicling for him)!

Just recently, Mom handed over the baby journal to me. In examining her many entries, it appears that, when I was two years old, two equally significant events occurred. The first was a cross-country move; the second was the arrival of my often-sickly little brother. The baby journal records that I spontaneously stopped eating almost immediately after these two occurrences. It also records that my parents were mystified as to why. Knowing what I know today about possible triggers for eating disorders, I can only assume that it was the stress of family life, and my parents' necessary shift in focus to include both me and my brother, that caused the sudden restrictive behaviors. But, for whatever reason, over the next three years, Mom's entries into the baby journal note increasingly frequent parental worries about my low food intake that prompted repeated visits to the family pediatrician. On each visit, my parents would complain about my small appetite and apparent low weight-to-height ratio. On each visit, the pediatrician would once again assure them that I was "just fine."

Today, a family physician might have a slightly less optimistic assessment. It is now known that individuals at risk for developing eating disorders tend to share similar personality traits to my own (intelligence, poor emotional coping skills, weak sense of self, perfectionist tendencies, and strong social conscience.) Furthermore, researchers have identified a Chromosome One genetic linkage for anorexia and a Chromosome 10P linkage for bulimia – a linkage that, basically, passes the DNA for eating disorders along like a water brigade from generation to generation. As a matter of fact, I find it less than coincidental that, on my dad's side of the family, an aunt and a female cousin continue to battle severe anorexia and bulimia. In other words, eating disorders are in my blood.

It is also now known that those who develop eating disorders often struggle a great deal to regroup from the aftershocks of change or trauma, like a sudden move, abuse of any kind, or the birth, death, or illness of a loved one. Just a few years later, at the age of six, I was sexually molested by an older neighborhood boy who had been hired to watch us while my parents went out for the evening. While I quickly "confessed" the molestation incident to my parents, the boy's warnings that telling "our secret" meant that I was the one at fault had already left their mark. I became deeply afraid of my developing body, and of my own apparent inability to safeguard it – and me – from harm.

At age ten, one year older than my classmates, and with the early onset of puberty making me one year taller and bigger as well, I entered middle school. A natural introvert, I was instantly intimidated by the milling crowds of strangers all around me. But my best friend Leslie was with me, so I reassured myself that I would at least have one friend to turn to. That quickly ended when Leslie approached me in the lunchroom one day and demanded to know if I had been "telling people we are friends." She explained that, in case I had not noticed, we were in middle school now, and she wanted to be popular. It turned out that she and her social aspirations had determined that I was too fat to fit into the social circle she wanted to belong to. So she asked me not to tell anyone else that we knew each other anymore. In shock, I mutely agreed.

Between my sixth and seventh grade year, bolstered by that still-painful memory, and with the unwitting support of my parents, I went on a "sensible diet" to lose my baby fat. My dad, who was just coming off of a successful diet himself, dieted with me to lend solidarity. I came back to middle school that fall standing five inches taller and many pounds lighter. Suddenly, classmates who would sooner bend down to pet a tree roach rather than acknowledge my existence were rushing up to me, flinging their arms around me, exclaiming about how good I looked and asking me how I did it! After auditioning and failing to make the exclusive performing choir in my sixth grade year, in my new, slimmer incarnation I suddenly won a spot in the All-Region choir and auditioned to win the lead role in not one, but TWO school plays.

I was hooked. This was it – I was convinced that I had found the holy grail of social acceptance. I was actually grateful for my newfound discovery – it was a breath of fresh air after a sixth grade year filled with abandonment, judgment, shame, and loneliness. Through weight loss, I had found a simple mechanism through which to filter all of the frightening unknowns that lay ahead. Because of this, I became determined to add a little extra "insurance" to my plan – I decided that, while I was on a roll, I would just lose a few more pounds now, and then later I would be able to eat whatever I wanted and everyone would love me.

As I doggedly went about implementing my plan, my mother changed her tune. Instead of continuing to encourage me in my attempts to adopt a slimming meal plan, she began begging me to eat more. I vividly remember turning my back to her one day and walking away, thinking deep within myself, "You do not understand. I cannot stop. Something has got me, and IT is in control now.'

I struggled with "IT" – aka the anorexia – for the next seven years. I had no name for my disease. I had no idea that I was not alone in battling an eating disorder. I had no clue that my inner hell was caused by anything other than "just me, being me." This ignorance was shared and widespread, as my weight loss and "food issues" became a constant source of stress and strain between me and my family, and me and my friends. Relationships disintegrated. I discovered the intense, solitary rigors of self-discipline, and applied all of my considerable energy, drive, and determination to two things, and only two things: restricting my food intake, and practicing my instruments until I was note-perfect. At the age of seventeen I won a national music contest, coming in second behind my own prodigiously talented teacher. Twice in the same year I was featured as an up-and-coming young jazz artist in a national jazz magazine. I was accepted to several prestigious music colleges, and entered one of them that fall as a freshman.

Barely three months later, I was back home again, sidelined for the foreseeable future due to severe, unexpected practice-related injuries to the tendons and ligaments in my hands. The doctors told my parents that they had never seen such a severe performance injury in one so young. They wrote in my case file that my injuries resembled those of a thirty-year career musician! They prescribed physical therapy, but stated that they were not sure I would ever recover to play at the same level again. Nobody talked about the fact that I wasn't using the on-campus cafeteria meal plan my parents had purchased for me.

And at that point, my world completely fell apart. I had no remaining identity outside of who I was when playing music. I decided that, if I could not play music, I no longer wanted to live.

The worst part was that I still had no idea what was wrong with me. My family was as clueless as I was. My mother shopped around for a physical therapist to try to at least salvage my music career. The woman she found, Annie*, became my first mentor. She was the first fresh and objective set of eyes to enter my life in quite some years, and maybe that was why she entered equipped and willing to see what the rest of us could or would not. She somehow gently coaxed details about my secret terror of food and fat out of me. She cooked scrambled eggs and buttered toast for me, and I would always eat, in spite of the fear, when she asked me to. Annie was the first person who taught me that there is a difference between the struggle and the person struggling. She also taught me that I had the right, and the worth, to stand up and FIGHT for my life.

Annie is a large part of the reason that I am alive and well today to tell my story. For the next several years, with her support, I began the slow, difficult, upward climb out of the pit of my eating disorder. My "progress," so to speak, was filled with relapses, pit stops, and false starts. For instance, in my sincere and well-intentioned efforts to begin eating again, I happened across purging as an alternative to restricting, and, in so doing, developed bulimia.

But this didn't faze Annie – she continued to stand firm in her belief that I was capable of finding the solution to any problem life presented to me, no matter how long it took or how many mistakes I made along the way. I continually drew strength from her as life got harder.

Annie also taught me to be very creative in problem-solving to meet my own stated recovery goals. In fact, one of the first things I did, with Annie's help, was to identify something I wanted more than my eating disorder – what I now call my "key to life." I decided that I wanted my music career back, and then I decided that I was willing to fight to the death to wrest it from the clutches of whatever had taken it from me, or die trying. Next, I taught myself to turn my own mind from my enemy into my ally – I learned how to coax it to want recovery as badly as I did. I then taught myself to turn my considerable resources of intelligence, discipline, determination, and perseverance away from perfecting my "eating behaviors" and toward overcoming them. Most importantly, from the start, I leaned into my relationship with my mentor, slowly but surely allowing her to guide me in how to replace my relationship with food with my relationship with people, one proven, trustworthy person at a time. In time, I even rediscovered the joy of developing a supportive relationship with myself!

Today, I share my experiences with others, believing wholeheartedly that *Relationships Replace Eating Disorders*. We all have something to teach, and something more to learn. We are never too sick to help someone else, or too well to accept help ourselves. I am happy to report that I have been virtually symptom-free for the last decade. I regained my music career, released two music CDs, and am now working on a third. I also recently released a book called *Beating Ana: How to Outsmart Your Eating Disorder and Take Your Life Back*, which outlines many of the techniques I developed to recover in lieu of access to professional treatment. Recently I even realized a dream I have held onto ever since I recovered, when, with the help of Andrea Roe and my own current mentor, Lynn, we launched *Mentor***CONNECT**, the first global online mentoring network created specifically to connect caring mentors in strong recovery with those who need one-on-one recovery support for eating disorders.

Add to that a wealth of close friends, a renewed closeness with my family, and as many goals, plans, and dreams as there are stars in the sky… none of which have anything to do with a number on the scale or reflection in the mirror… and there you have it – a true-to-life picture of life after anorexia and bulimia.

It is good to be alive. I LIKE my life. I like ME! And I am very thankful for my recovery. I would not be the person I am today, or have the life I have now, without it. In the years I spent recovering, I learned that we all have something – something that we struggle with, something we must overcome in order to learn the lessons life wants to teach us. And, while I do recognize that every person's experiences and circumstances are unique, I continue to remain convinced that any person who wants recovery as badly as I wanted it, and is willing to work as hard as their own recovery process demands, can also overcome their "something" to achieve recovery and reclaim their right to a healthy, happy, fulfilling life – just like I did.

If I could do it, then SO CAN YOU. There is always something more you can do to save your own life. And there is never, EVER, a reason to give up!

Shannon Cutts is the author of *Beating Ana: How to Outsmart Your Eating Disorder and Take Your Life Back* (Health Communications, Inc.) and founder of Key to Life: unlocking the door to hope, an organization that provides programs, workshops, concerts, products, and services to foster awareness, education, intervention, and prevention of eating and related disorders. More recently, Shannon founded MentorCONNECT, the first global mentoring network to connect those in strong recovery from eating disorders with those who need recovery support. For more information about Shannon and her work, visit www.key-to-life.com

* Name has been changed to protect the person's privacy.

Shannon's songs, *My Mask* and *You Are Not Alone* are featured on the *You Are Not Alone Companion CD.*

Finding My True Self and Inner Beauty

By Andrea Roe

My name is Andrea. I am twenty-seven years old and a recovered anorexic and bulimic. I am Austrian, married to a wonderful Canadian and currently living in beautiful British Columbia, Canada. I struggled with eating disorders for six long years and have finally overcome these deadly diseases – and this is my story…

While I was growing up, food and weight were not a problem for me. I came from a very active and health-oriented family and never had to worry about my weight. Almost every weekend my parents would take my siblings and me walking, hiking, biking, or skiing or on a sightseeing trip to a gorgeous place somewhere in Austria. I like thinking about my childhood; it was a wonderful time, and thinking about it creates a warm feeling inside of me. Even now, while I am writing this, I have a smile on my face and a tear of joy in my eyes.

When I was about thirteen-years old, someone said to me that my face looked weird when I smiled, and then she started to laugh. She said this in front of other people. I was very confused; I did not know what to say, and I blushed. I had never paid much attention to my smile until that day. When I came home from school, I looked at myself in the mirror. I smiled. I used two mirrors and looked at my smile from different angles. I stared at myself for hours, and, came to the conclusion that the girl was right. My smile was ugly! And I looked ugly when I smiled. I decided not to smile anymore.

It took almost ten years before I learned to love my smile again. In photographs taken during those years, I hardly ever smiled. (By the way, this comment did not cause my eating disorder; it is an example of the power of words, and how one simple innocent comment can spiral out of control). That happened about two or three years before my eating disorder developed. It was the first step towards disliking and hating my face, and eventually my body.

Around that time, I also developed acne. I already did not like my face because of my "ugly" smile, and having blemished skin made me hate my face even more. I tried everything that was on the market to get rid of my skin problems, but nothing helped. I became depressed and cried a lot. I started wearing makeup to cover the red spots. I would not leave the house without putting it on, so ashamed was I of my face. There were times I did not go to school because of my skin; I did not want anyone to look at it. I did not like people looking at me, at my skin. I did not want them to look at what was "wrong" with me.

My parents did everything in their power to help, support, and comfort me. They were always there for me. I had times when I cried almost every day and locked myself in my room. I just wanted to be alone. I would lie on my bed, look at my face in a mirror and cry. Not many people knew about those struggles, or how big a problem my skin really was for me. I was a very sad teenage girl on the inside, but did not show this to other people. I pretended to be strong.

When I was fifteen, I had the thought that I had to lose some weight. There was no reason for me to go on a diet, but I felt so badly about myself and I thought maybe losing some weight would make me feel better about myself. I wanted to feel pretty and was desperate to do anything to feel that way, and I thought losing weight might be a way to get there. I felt like I had nothing to lose; I already hated myself and what I looked liked so much… things just could not get any worse for me, but they did…

My dieting got out of control, and I slipped into having an eating disorder – I had developed anorexia. I do not know exactly when my eating disorder started and my dieting ended, I just slipped into it.

I read a lot of women's magazines and adored the female models in those magazines – their beautiful smiles, their clear skin, and their flawless bodies. Back then I did not know that what I looked at, what I admired and wanted to look like, was not real but digitally airbrushed and drastically altered by computers. At that point, I did not know that I had a problem. I was in denial, and I thought that what I was doing was normal. Now, when I look back, I can see how much I was already into my eating disorder world. I just did not notice it back then.

I was the only one in my group of friends who did not have a boyfriend, and I felt weird about it. It was proof that there was indeed something wrong with me, and I knew exactly what it was – it must have been because I was ugly; it must have been because of my smile and my skin.

Sometimes when lying in bed at night, I imagined how life would be if I liked my face, smile, and body. How "easy" life would be because I would not have to hide anymore. I would not have to be afraid of people looking at me anymore. I could be free of all my worries! I would be happy.

After graduating at eighteen, I went to university. The idea of me not being beautiful was still stuck in my head. It was at this point that my eating disorder started to take complete control of my life.

I started binging in order to try to fill the emptiness inside of me, although I never threw up. I wanted to so much, but for some reason I was not able to make myself vomit. Instead, I would use other methods to get rid of the food and the calories quickly, like over-exercising and diet pill and laxative abuse. I would eat until my stomach started to ache. I felt disgusted with myself and what I was doing. I was very ashamed and embarrassed about my behaviour. For the longest time I did not tell anyone about my problem and struggled on my own, secretly and in silence.

Unfortunately, my eating disorder did not stop there. It not only changed my relationship with food and weight, it started taking control over my social life as well. I did not go out for a coffee, lunch, or dinner with my friends anymore. I felt uncomfortable eating in front of other people. I did not want anyone to force me to eat. I was terrified by the thought of gaining weight. I also feared that they would notice what was going on with me. I was afraid of them asking questions. I did not want anyone to find out what I was doing, and lied a lot to my friends in order to keep my eating disorder a secret. I did not like lying to them but I felt I had no other choice. I thought that if they knew they would not like me anymore and would not want to be friends with me.

During the first couple of years of my struggles, I was not very educated about eating disorders, mainly because I was in denial for so long. I knew only a bit of basic information and had no idea about where to get useful information about eating disorders, where to turn for help – I was too shy to ask. I thought that one had to be either extremely skinny or extremely heavy in order to be taken seriously, but I was neither. My weight was always somewhere in the normal healthy weight range. And people with eating disorders have to be one of those extremes, do they not?

I eventually hit a point where I could not deny my problem any longer and was finally able to admit to myself that what I was doing was not healthy and that I needed to stop this behaviour. But I did not know what to do or where to start. I felt lost and confused, and thought I was the only one who had this problem.

I did not know how to get out of my eating disorder cycle. I was ruining not only my mind and health, but also my life. I was hurting not only myself but also the people around me. Many nights I would cry myself to sleep, wondering if I was ever going to recover – or if there even was such a thing as "recovery."

I had always had a very close relationship with my parents, but my eating disorder forced me to move away from them. I became very reserved and quiet. They knew what was going on and hoped I would talk to them so they could support and help me. Sometimes I wanted to tell them about my struggles, I wanted to be taken in their arms; I wanted to feel that I was loved no matter what. I thought about talking to them for months but was never sure what to say. I was afraid of disappointing them. I wanted them to be proud of me. But how could they be proud of me when I had an eating disorder?

I eventually opened up to my mum. I gave her a book about how to deal with someone who struggles with an eating disorder, and wrote a letter to her as well. I could see how relieved she was that I finally opened up to her, and she took me in her arms and comforted me. I was crying a lot on that day but I was glad I told her.

My eating disorder did not get better after my conversation with my mum, but at least I knew now that I had someone to talk to when I needed help, comfort, and support.

After I told my mum, I went to a therapist. The therapist did not specialize in eating disorders – she was a general therapist. I was so nervous about calling her that it took me several days until I was ready to call her office and set up an appointment.

My appointment was on a sunny afternoon in spring. I was nineteen-years old. I remember sitting in her office and telling her my life story. She sat opposite me, on the other side of the desk, listening to what I had to say and making a lot of notes. I told her about my smile, my skin, my eating disorder and how it changed my behaviour, and my relationship with my family and friends. I also talked to her about my issues of not having a boyfriend and that, while on the one hand I wanted to have a boyfriend so much, on the other hand I was afraid of letting anyone close to me and letting anyone touch me.

When I started talking about the boyfriend issue, she asked me if I had had sex. I said no. I was surprised by her asking this question and felt somewhat uncomfortable. She asked me why I did not have sex. I said that I did not because I did not have a boyfriend. She told me that sex feels good and that I would like it and that I should think about having it. I did not like her asking these questions and making these comments. What did it matter to her if I slept with someone or not? I was not there to talk about sex; I was there to figure out my life, to get healthy again. I found her comments rude and inappropriate, and I was offended.

At the end of the session, she gave me a business card of another specialist and told me to call him. She said that I was "too advanced" for her, "too deep in my eating disorder that she could not help me anymore." After she said that, the appointment was over. I left her office, totally confused. I did not know what to think. I felt discouraged. I felt like a hopeless case. I never called the other therapist; I did not want to waste any more money on a therapist just to hear that I was "too messed up to get help."

For the next two years I continued my self-destructive path of bulimia. But no matter how much food I ate, I was not able to fill the emptiness inside me. I wasted so much money on food; I do not even want to think about the amount I spent on my binges. I withdrew socially, even more than I had before; I had spent most of my time alone, either eating, over-exercising, or starving myself. I led a lonely and sad life and had little hope about ever getting better. I spent so much time in my room alone, escaping into the virtual world of my computer. Here I was safe; nobody was able to see me, to judge me or hurt me. I know my parents were very worried about me, but they had no idea how to get close to me. When they tried, they were not successful. I did not let anyone get close. I completely shut them out. I cried almost every day, sometimes even a couple of times a day.

What had happened to me? How could I have let it come that far? I felt completely hopeless. I wanted to get better and be happy and healthy again...but I did not even know where to start my journey towards recovery. Besides, I was not even sure if there was such a thing as "recovery."

Just looking at myself in the mirror made me cry. I hated my face, my body, everything. There was nothing pretty about me. Even though my skin had improved and became really nice over time, and I had stopped wearing makeup to cover up my face, I did not recognize that nor was I grateful for it. Even though my acne was gone, it still did not change the fact that I hated my face – and my smile.

My turning point came when I met a wonderful man from Canada who is now my husband. We met in London, England, and it was love at first sight. We immediately felt a special bond, and it seemed as if we had known one another for a long time already. It almost felt like "coming home." It felt wonderful to be close to him. I felt safe. He was also my first boyfriend. I finally had what I had desired for so long – a loving, caring, and understanding man by my side who truly and deeply loved me.

In the beginning, I did not tell him about my eating disorder. I was afraid that if he found out he would leave me, and I did not want him to. I was afraid of being alone again. When I was around him, I would eat normally, and it felt good. For the first time in years I felt "normal." I decided to move to Canada with him, and we moved in together, very quickly, which, in the long run, really helped me with my eating disorder.

Moving to Canada meant another dream of mine came true. For years I had wanted to move abroad and spend some time in another country. When I was fourteen, I had gone to England with two friends for three weeks to improve my poor English. I really enjoyed it there and fell in love with the language. At that point I decided I wanted to marry someone who spoke English; I wanted to speak English in my relationship – I just loved the way the language sounded!

Over the next couple of years, I sometimes told my friends about my dream of moving abroad and marrying someone who spoke English. I do not know if they took me seriously, but deep inside I was serious. This dream did not only have to do with the language. Over the years, while struggling with eating disorders, my desire to live abroad became stronger and stronger. I wanted to travel, I wanted to live someplace else (somewhere they spoke English, though). I thought that with moving away, I would be able to leave all my problems behind and start over – without my eating disorder. I thought I would finally be free. I would be happy.

I could not have been more wrong. I was so looking forward to moving to Canada, to starting over, to creating a "better" life. I had so many plans but nothing had changed. Running away from my problems did not work. And why should it? I could not run away from them. I never would be able to, because the real "problem" was me.

I still binged, but I was not able to do it as often because I only binged when I was alone, and, since Brandon and I lived together, we spent a lot of time together. He never noticed my binges, but he did notice that I had stomachaches on a regular basis, and he worried about me. I always told him I had problems adjusting to the food in Canada and that was where my stomachaches came from. He never doubted what I said and never acted suspicious. He saw no reason to; why would I lie to him? But I did lie to him, and I lied a lot. I felt like I had to, as if I had no other choice. I did not want him to find out what was really going on with me. I was afraid of losing him, of being left alone.

It took me a couple of months until I was ready to tell him about what was going on with me. He had not even noticed and seemed quite surprised. Brandon took me in his arms, gave me a kiss and said that we would get through this together, and that he would always be there for me and do whatever it took to get me healthy again. I started crying. It felt as if a heavy weight had been lifted off my shoulders. He believed in me, in us, and he believed that together we would be able to beat this disorder. For the first time in years, I felt, just maybe, recovery was possible for me.

Today, I am healthy. I am grateful for my body, and I love myself and my life. I am thankful that my body has not given up on me after many years of abuse.

My journey to recovery was difficult at times. I had to take it one day after the other. I had setbacks; I had a lot of them. Every time I fell, I got up again and continued on my journey. I did my best not to look back, but forward.

Brandon was always there for me and with me, every step of the way. We talked a lot and I told him everything, and I mean EVERYTHING. There were a lot of things I told him that were not pretty, but, no matter what I said, his feelings for me did not get any less. He never judged me or my behaviour, no matter what I did. The only thing he did not want me to do was to lie to him and cover up things. It was important for him that I always told him the truth, no matter how "bad" it was. That was one of the hardest patterns for me to break – to stop lying. I had been lying about my eating behaviour for so many years that I did not even notice it anymore when I did… lying just happened automatically.

My husband also taught me to smile again. He always told me that I looked pretty when I smiled and that I was a beautiful girl. I did not believe him at first, but over time I was able to see that I really was beautiful girl, inside and out, with a beautiful smile. Now, I actually love my smile. I did not smile for pictures in almost ten years, and these days, whenever pictures are taken, I am the first one to smile!

I am so thankful for having Brandon in my life. He has always been there for me; he has always believed in me and never gave up on me. His love and support are what I needed to find the strength in me to beat this disorder.

I have reached the point where I am able to openly and honestly talk about my eating disorder struggles and everything connected with it. I am not ashamed anymore of my past and no longer feel the need to hide it. I always saw my eating disorder as something negative, as "lost years." Now, I can see it in a positive way. If not for my past, I know I would not be who I am today and would not be where I am today – and I like the person I am, and I love my life.

I believe very strongly that everything happens for a reason, even though often we are unable to see the reason right away. While I was struggling, I often asked myself what good reason all this pain, all these tears, could possibly have, and I never found an answer. Now, things have started to fall into place and make sense. All of it was a big learning experience for me, one that was necessary to make me the person I am now. It was a painful and difficult experience, that is for sure, but it was necessary. I have learned so much over the past few years, about life and about myself that I would not have otherwise. I now know who I am. I have found my place in life. I have found personal meaning in my life.

My life is not about me anymore. For years I was a lonely and depressed girl who lived a small, sad life. Now I have the desire to make a difference in other people's lives and want to give back to society. It is my passion to show others who are struggling with eating disorders that there is a way out, and that these disorders can be beaten.

I want you to know that it **IS** possible to recover. **Please do not give up on yourself. You CAN get through this!** I know – I did it, and so can you! Your eating disorder did not just happen overnight, it started a long time ago, before you first binged, purged or starved yourself. It will take time to get better, one step at a time.

Eating disorders are not simply about food and weight. They are an attempt to use food and weight to deal with emotional problems. An eating disorder is just a symptom of something deeper going on inside of you. Food and your body are not the enemy, even though it sometimes feels like it. You can learn to enjoy your life again. Please keep on believing in yourself and continue to be strong.

You are a beautiful human being. One day, I know you will be able to see it!

Andrea Roe struggled with eating disorders for six years, and now that she is recovered, it is her passion to support others in their struggles. She released her first book entitled *You Are Not Alone – The Book of Companionship for Women Struggling with Eating Disorders (Volume I)* in 2006, and is the publisher of the *You Are Not Alone Support Letter*, a monthly email newsletter filled with recovery stories, poems, artwork, and more. Andrea also travels and shares her story with students and patients in treatment centres in Canada and the US.

For more information about Andrea and her work, and to get in touch with her, visit www.youarenotalonebook.com

Song Lyrics – You Are Not Alone Companion CD

You Are Not Alone

By Shannon Cutts

She can hear the cries
But she don't know where they're coming from
The shadowed sighs – they don't sound of this world
She can hear them when she's sleeping
They greet her when she wakes
No one can silence what she aches for and is afraid to name

Come out and show yourself and see you are not alone
I am just me – you are just you – and you are not alone
You are not alone
You are not alone

Tired eyes
From one more night of sleep, not sleeping
On the inside – working overtime
Can it be figured out
Can she outlive herself
Find strength in places she's afraid to go – afraid to face

Come out and show yourself and see you are not alone
I am just me – you are just you – and you are not alone
You are not alone
You are not alone

Shannon Cutts is the author of *Beating Ana: How to Outsmart Your Eating Disorder and Take Your Life Back* (Health Communications, Inc.) and founder of Key to Life: unlocking the door to hope, an organization that provides programs, workshops, concerts, products, and services to foster awareness, education, intervention, and prevention of eating and related disorders. More recently, Shannon founded MentorCONNECT, the first global mentoring network to connect those in strong recovery from eating disorders with those who need recovery support. For more information about Shannon and her work, visit www.key-to-life.com

Words & Music by Shannon Cutts

www.key-to-life.com

This song has to do with staying strong in the face of demands from someone I loved to conform to narrow views of beauty.

My Shape

By Jenny Dalton

The sun is getting lower
the air turns slightly crisper
your warmth is leaving my body
I hate the sound of fading
can't stand the shape you're drawing
surprised to see us still mortal

But I am not afraid to let go

I am so sorry to hear that
your holy war is over
just when you decided to fight
Something cold and shallow
found its home in your wiring
Hard wiring can be so lethal

But I am not afraid to let go

It turns me over and over
but I feel freedom coming on.
Do you wish I was more fragile? Do you want to break me?
Do you wish I was more pliable? Do you want to bend me?
Do you wish I was more fragile? So you want to break me?
Do you wish I was more pliable?
Do you want to change my shape?

Jenny Dalton is twenty-nine years old and lives in Minneapolis, Minnesota. She is a singer, pianist, songwriter, and recording artist. Jenny defies pressures to maintain an unhealthy image and nurtures a creative lifestyle through care of the mind, body and soul. For more information about Jenny and her music, visit www.jennydalton.com

Words & Music by Jenny Dalton

www.jennydalton.com

The Good You Do

By Christine Kane

You say that in times like these
You're driven down to your knees
Looking around grieving what peace there was
You promised yourself you would
Work for a world of good
Look at you now wondering what good it does

No lost hope no violent point of view
Can erase all of the good you do

There's nothing as dark as night
But nothing so strong as light
Here is the choice: to let it burn out or bright
In a world where the fear and force
Have buried the silent source
Can you deny the need for a light like yours

No fast pace no jaded attitude
Can erase all of the good you do

If someone has left his wrath
On everything in his path
Taking the wealth and leaving his trash behind
Will you be peace or pride
Can you at last decide
There's no one to fight we are the same inside

So go home and get some rest
There's many more miles and tests
All about love what if it comes to be all that we have left

No dark place no debt and no abuse
Can erase all of the good you do

Christine Kane, from Asheville, NC, healed from a ten-year bout with bulimia and went on to create a successful music career. She has been writing and performing her songs nationally for thirteen years. Two national dance companies have choreographed ballets to Christine's music, and her songs have been recorded by popular artists, including Kathy Mattea and "Nashville Star" finalist Casey Simpson. *The Washington Post* called her "a petite powerhouse of a singer." She is also sought-after as a teacher and speaker, praised for her humorous and authentic approach to creativity and goal setting. For more information about Christine, visit www.christinekane.com

Words & Music by Christine Kane

www.christinekane.com

I wrote this song right after the Katrina hurricane as a reminder to myself to always be grateful for what I have instead of feeling I need more to be happy.

Lucky

By Halie Loren

I have a bowl of fruit
A sink that rarely leaks
When I breathe I fill my lungs with air that's sweet
I have a soft bed
A closet full of clothes
When I step outside its on soil where grass can grow

And I have, I have, I have, I have…
Enough
And I need, I need, I need, I need…
Nothing else much, I'm

Lucky – this a lucky life
I see it more and more how
Lucky is a relative state of mind
And as long as I concede
That I've got all that I need
To be satisfied, I'll feel lucky
All my life

I have a friend to call
A sister to worry about me
When I fall, I know someone will help me get back on my feet

And I have, I have, I have, I have, I have…
More than I know
And I need, I need, I need, I need, I need…
Nothing else to show I'm

Lucky – this is a lucky life
I see it more and more how

Lucky is a relative state of mind
And as long as I concede that I've got all that I need to be satisfied
I'll feel lucky all my life.

Sometimes when times get hard it's hard to believe
Life's not a dry well
But seeing what fades, what lasts, gives me reason to remind myself…
Lucky is a state of mind
My friend, I'm so

Lucky – this is a lucky life
I see it more and more how
Lucky is a relative state of mind
And as long as I concede
That I've got all that I need
To be satisfied, I'll feel lucky
All my life.

I have a bowl of fruit….

Halie Loren is twenty-four-years old and lives in Eugene, Oregon. She is a singer, pianist, songwriter, recording artist, and recipient of several music awards. Halie struggled with eating disorders and negative body image for several years, and is now recovered. After winning her fight with eating disorders, she released her first solo album, *Full Circle* at the age of twenty-two. For more information about Halie and her music, visit www.halieloren.com

"I would like to hear that listeners would gain some feeling of empowerment from my music. This particular album was certainly an empowering project for me to create… and extremely cathartic, too. When it comes down to it, this album was all about exorcising all these different emotional holdings I had been ignoring or subconsciously unaware of for quite a while. Many of the songs were a result of my really opening up and being honest with myself, facing down hurtful experiences, frustrations, and emotional hardships that I'd never allowed myself to fully process. The process also delivered a lot of epiphanies about the wonderful, joyful things that I hadn't fully acknowledged--the things taken for granted, or that require broader perspective to truly understand in the greater context of things. It was this that led to writing "Lucky," my favorite song on the album. So it was only in writing about feelings of abandonment, resentment, about my past struggles with eating disorders and body image, and also in tapping into a new well of gratitude that I could feel that pressure release. It is in sharing, or at least expressing, our experiences that we can truly either let them go or finally embrace them as a part of who we are. Either way is extremely liberating, and can deliver profound emotional healing." – *Halie Loren*

Words & Music by Halie Loren (Smith)

http://www.halieloren.net

Guardian Angel

By Christene LeDoux

And I don't know why it is you believe
you need to starve yourself or throw up
to look like some girl on the cover of a magazine
when all you really want is love

don't you know who you are
when you move your body to dance
or strum your guitar

when you fall to pick yourself up
I don't see the problem
you've got lungs so you can breathe

If I could be your guardian angel
I'd give you wings so you could fly
maybe then you'd see
maybe then you'd believe
you're an angel in disguise

one hundred and one reasons to give up
not one to put up
the fight you're always bragging about

what are you bragging about anyway
anyone can throw in the towel

you say you like my songs
well listen to this one
every word to you is tough love

I can't sit on the outside
I can't sit on the outside
I can't sit on the outside
and watch as you dissolve

If I could be your guardian angel
I'd give you wings so you could fly
maybe then you'd see
maybe then you'd believe
you're an angel in disguise

maybe then you'd see
maybe then you'd believe
you're an angel to me

Christene LeDoux began her career in San Francisco and lived everywhere in between before settling in Innsbruck, Austria. This award-winning songwriter and gifted storyteller, tours full-time around the world. Along her travels she met a friend who would later inspire her song, *Guardian Angel.* It was written after witnessing this friend practicing bulimia, and is just one example of Christene's tireless efforts to facilitate healing and peace through her music. For more information, visit
www.christeneledoux.com

Words & Music by Christene LeDoux

We Are Who We Are

By Alexandra Kelly

We spend our lives
On the outside looking in
We feel like strangers, inside our own skin
But look at the people
That you know and who you love
And they'll say

You are perfect as you are
And I hope you never ever change
You are perfect as you are
I hope you stay the same
Cause we are who we are

We live these ordinary lives
Day by day
Not knowing where we fit
Or what we're supposed to say
But here I stand my heart in my hands
And I believe
That every word I say
Will somehow make you see
What we see

You are perfect as you are
And I hope you never ever change
You are perfect as you are
I hope you stay the same
Cause we are who we are

We've all taken chances
Let a moment pass by
Let life slip through our fingers
Without asking why
I want you to stop look around you
See the beauty in time

I want you to spread your wings
Spread your wings and fly

You are perfect as you are
And I hope you never ever change
You are perfect as you are
I hope you stay the same
Cause we are who we are

Alexandra Kelly lives in Fair Lawn, NJ. Just eighteen-years old, she has numerous awards and honours already under her belt, including an invitation to work with Grammy-nominated artists as part of the Grammy Foundation Program, a summer program for teenage music artists, in 2007 and 2008. She wrote *We Are Who We Are* for a good friend who is recovering from an eating disorder. For more information about Alexandra and her music, visit www.alexandrakelly.com

Words & Music by Alexandra Kelly

bodyMINE

By Lori B

I was schooled to scorn the flesh
I learned to love the bone
Chasing magazine silhouettes
I disowned my own

Sweet vessel, bodyMine
Won't you be my home?
We've been separated too long

I'm a veteran of this endless
Siege against myself
Don't know how this war got started
I just fought like hell

Sweet vessel, bodyMine
Won't you be my home?
We've been separated too long

How can I undo what's done?
Heal the ancient wound
For so long this bodySong
Was full of pain and full of shame

Now I hear a different voice
Calling sweet and low
Telling me that I have been set free

Sweet vessel, bodyMine
I've been so alone
Praise the day you welcomed me
Back home

Praise the day you welcomed me
Praise the day you welcomed me
Praise the day you welcomed me

Back home

Sweet vessel, bodyMine

Lori B lives in San Francisco and is a survivor of eating disorders. After a stint in the film business, she trained and practiced as a body-centered psychotherapist in New York City. She has performed and taught various kinds of healing, dancing, music and ritual in theaters and living rooms around the world. For more information about her music, photography, writing and private coaching work, please visit www.loriB.net

Words & Music by Lori B

www.lorib.net

Skin

By Jennifer Friedman

Time
until death
do us part
until death
do they chart
our beloved life

and what doctors
regard as charm she says is
western hunger for blood money
or so is my humble interpretation of an
ordinary girl

who swears she doesn't have half my brain
coulda' fooled me
for blood money is statistically red
and manufactured green

my skin your skin is real is real
my skin your skin is real is real
my skin your skin is real is real
my skin your skin my skin

gray is the hair
of a lady who saves
her color
for cloudy days

and the touch
of your hand
not enough
to withstand
the fire that they swear's just warm embrace

and the reasons

not to abide
are heaven hell and earth aside
so you find another god with which to pray

and when that one and her dreams and answers are
tooth fairy santa tales
you close your eyes and wish the world away

my skin your skin is real is real
my skin your skin is real is real
my skin your skin is real is real
my skin your skin my skin

my skin your skin is real is real
my skin your skin is real is real
my skin your skin is real is real
my skin your skin my skin

and no matter how chewed up, tired, pink or gray or battered perspired
no matter how guilty the priest who was my father was my friend
no matter how indecent the touch that made you a statistic
i am still the rightful owner of my skin

there are pores
that exist
just to soak
in the sound
of running water and the hymns of midnight jazz

there are abstract
joys and understandings
that increase indefinitely over the years

and with age
come anger like
fire come heat
when you learn to lure the barrel up the ever-threatening peak

and to wear
sweet armor when

touching fire
so as not to burn love falling at your feet

my skin your skin is real is real
my skin your skin is real is real
my skin your skin is real is real
my skin your skin my skin

Jennifer Friedman, a New York native and graduate of SUNY Purchase, first discovered her love for music as a little girl sitting at her parents' piano. She overcame an eating disorder to record an album of her original songs and begin performing them. For more information about Jennifer, visit www.jennfriedman.com and www.myspace.com/jennfriedman

Words & Music by Jennifer Friedman

www.myspace.com/jennfriedman

STRoNG eNouGH

By Heather Purdin

Well you chewed me up when you let me in
Just to spit me out
And you left me here, yeah you left me here
With just my skin to bare.
(My skin to bare)

(Not a seed to sew, not a row to hoe
Just an empty hole).
And well it wasn't much, no it wasn't much
But just enough
(To wake me up).

So i could see all the things
i still need from me.

CHORUS:
And that my only true enemy
is just a reflection of me.
And that's alright
i think i'm strong enough
To stand on my own two feet
And let my courage carry me.
To lick my own wounds and let
Time heal the rest.
***** ***** *****

i let your powder friend here bait me in
To your messed up world
And we were flying high and dropping low
it won't let you go
(Won't let you go)

i'm facing memories in hopes that they'll
Stop haunting me.
Oh remember when you crossed the line

Between yours and mine
(Yours and mine)

but you helped me see all the things
i still need from me.

[CHORUS]

Heather Purdin, from Boone, NC, is a survivor of an eating disorder and experiences music as a powerful force for healing, a blessing she discovered after buying a guitar during her recovery process. She has a post-masters certificate in expressive arts therapy and will be doing some individual studies soon. Heather also finds time in her busy schedule to go on tour and sing and play keyboards with a reggae/funk band, Selah Dubb. For more information about Heather, and to get in touch with her, visit www.myspace.com/heatherpurdin or www.myspace.com/babybeatsreggae

Words & Music by Heather Purdin

www.myspace.com/heatherpurdin

The Angels Came

By Robin Richardson

It'll come around so they say
The world will turn around until one day
You will be the one to hold somebody else's hand
Keep their head above the quicksand

Look into my eyes you'll see
I am just the same
When I'd finally given up
The angels came

I know your life is hard
And that you've lost your faith
So just take my hand and let me lead you from this place
Soon you'll be the one to touch somebody else's life
And with a word of love show them that the world is kind

Look into my eyes you'll see
I am just the same
When I'd finally given up
The angels came

Robin Richardson, from Boulder, Colorado, is recovering from anorexia, bulimia, and alcoholism. She is also an incest survivor who is now thriving in her life. A singer-songwriter and inspirational speaker for all age groups, Robin is also a psychotherapist working with disordered eating, sexual abuse, and addictions. Robin's newest CD, *Wild Bird*, chronicles her journey out of addiction and despair into peace, self-love, and a life worth living. *Wild Bird* is available on www.sunlightofthespirit.com.
For more information about Robin, visit www.robinrichardson.net

"As many of us know, music can lend us a voice to describe deep feelings and inner pain that may be difficult to verbalize. Early in my career as a music therapist, I recognized the healing power of music with the eating disorder population. I realized that many women had the desire to express their thoughts and feelings, but just couldn't find the right words. I also recognized that many of my clients could more readily express their feelings through symbolic or metaphoric methods, such as art, poetry, or music. I decided to start teaching basic song writing techniques and see what happened. Though many of my clients have had no formal music training, they were able to write very touching lyrics, and eventually melodies that beautifully expressed their struggles during the recovery process and their hope for the future. 'My Choice' is one of many songs written, performed, and recorded entirely by courageous women who wanted their voices to be heard. I hope it touches your heart as much as it has mine."

My Choice

By Lynette Taylor and the Center for Change Women's Choir

How my heart aches to understand
The pain I grip within my hand
The good, the bad, the right, the wrong
Which one am I, which is my song?

Chorus:
But is this battle all in vain?
Or do I choose to face the pain?
I look inside and I find my voice
I want to live this is my choice

Not knowing what's exactly real
How can I battle what I feel?
Every breath's a constant strain
Fighting the depths of inner shame

Chorus

These tears I cry with secret meaning

A constant struggle of simply being
No longer will my fingers play
Those keys of sorrow from yesterday

Bridge:
Despite the darkness surrounding me
There's a light ahead to set me free
Looking for a new beginning
A wondrous thought of finally winning

Chorus 2:
Free to laugh and free to dream
My mended heart just wants to sing
Through the clouds I finally see
The sunshine starts to shine on me

I want to live this is my choice

Lynette Taylor resides in Salt Lake City, UT. She works as a Board-Certified Music Therapist at Center for Change (CFC), an inpatient treatment center for eating disorders. Lynette works to help women find hope in recovery through music. She is also the Director of the CFC Women's Choir. The song, *My Choice* was written and performed entirely by clients of CFC under Lynette's direction. For more information about Lynette and the CFC Women's Choir, visit www.centerforchange.com

Words & Music by Center for Change clients and staff members
CFC Women's Choir Directed by Lynette L. Taylor, MT-BC

www.centerforchange.com

This Mask

By Shannon Cutts

Behind this mask I am someone real
Behind my smile I'm afraid to feel
Too much hope - oh I can't breathe
When I dream of breaking free

From this mask my mother wore
She taught me well and at her door
Before goodbye she said to me
Take this mask my legacy but

I am beautiful though no one ever sees me
I pass the women on the streets and I know they feel the same
We are beautiful and if we stand together
We can let the masks fall at our feet

Without this mask I shut my eyes
Will the world cave in -- oh, will I die?
And it's this fear that's killing me
As I dream of breaking free

Without this mask I feel the sun
Caress my feet and warm my womb
Open my hands - accept the grace
That frees me from this great charade cause

I am beautiful though no one ever sees me
I pass the women on the streets and I know they feel the same
We are beautiful and if we stand together
We can let the masks fall at our feet

Shannon Cutts is the author of *Beating Ana: How to Outsmart Your Eating Disorder and Take Your Life Back* (Health Communications, Inc.) and founder of Key to Life: unlocking the door to hope, an organization that provides programs, workshops, concerts, products, and services to foster awareness, education, intervention, and prevention of eating and related disorders. More recently, Shannon founded MentorCONNECT, the first global mentoring network to connect those in strong recovery from eating disorders with those who need recovery support. For more information about Shannon and her work, visit www.key-to-life.com

Words & Music by Shannon Cutts

www.key-to-life.com

List of Contributors

In Alphabetical Order:

Alexandra Kelly lives in Fair Lawn, NJ. Just eighteen-years old, she has numerous awards and honors already under her belt, including an invitation to work with Grammy-nominated artists as part of the Grammy Foundation Program, a summer program for teenage music artists, in 2007 and 2008. She wrote *We Are Who We Are* for a good friend who is recovering from an eating disorder. For more information about Alexandra and her music, visit www.alexandrakelly.com

Andrea Roe struggled with eating disorders for six years and now that she is recovered, it is her passion to support others in their struggles. She released her first book entitled *You Are Not Alone – The Book of Companionship for Women Struggling with Eating Disorders (Volume I)* in 2006, and is the publisher of the *You Are Not Alone Support Letter*, a monthly email newsletter filled with recovery stories, poems, artwork, and more. Andrea also travels and shares her story with students and patients in treatment centers in Canada and the US. For more information about Andrea and her work, and to get in touch with her, visit www.youarenotalonebook.com

Angela Minard, who is married with four sons, is forty-years-old and lives in the United States. She has struggled with an eating disorder for many years, and is now in recovery. She is also a childhood rape survivor. If you want to get in touch with Angela, you can send an e-mail to angminard@kc.surewest.net or visit her website at www.poetrypoem.com/4angel

Cat S. Ginn is forty-seven-years-old and has struggled with an eating disorder for most of her life, but was not diagnosed as anorexic until around her fortieth birthday. Cat, who is also bipolar and a survivor of childhood sexual abuse, has been married for over twenty-five years to a wonderful man, and she is a loving mother to two children, aged twenty and fifteen. Cat, who has a BS in Art and Marketing, has written poetry and created art pieces since the age of four. Her lifelong dream is to publish her own poetry book and to sell her art. She has the love and support of her family and her best friend, Mutt. She is currently in therapy with a wonderful therapist on a weekly basis and has been at normal weight for about five years... and though she still hears Ed's voice (the eating disorder voice) inside her head, she considers herself in recovery and winning.

Christene LeDoux began her career in San Francisco and lived everywhere in between before settling in Innsbruck, Austria. This award-winning songwriter and gifted storyteller, tours full-time around the world. Along her travels she met a friend who would later inspire her song *Guardian Angel*. It was written after witnessing this friend practicing bulimia, and is just one example of Christene's tireless efforts to facilitate healing and peace through her music. For more information, visit www.christeneledoux.com

Christine Kane, from Asheville, NC, healed from a ten-year bout with bulimia and went on to create a successful music career. She has been writing and performing her songs nationally for thirteen years. Two national dance companies have choreographed ballets to Christine's music, and her songs have been recorded by popular artists, including Kathy Mattea and "Nashville Star" finalist Casey Simpson. *The Washington Post* called her "a petite powerhouse of a singer." She is also sought-after as a teacher and speaker, praised for her humorous and authentic approach to creativity and goal setting. For more information about Christine, visit www.christinekane.com

Erin Brinkle is nineteen years old and lives in Texas. She is recovering from a two-year battle with anorexia.

Halie Loren is twenty-four-years old and lives in Eugene, Oregon. She is a singer, pianist, songwriter, recording artist, and recipient of several music awards. Halie struggled with eating disorders and negative body image for several years, and is now recovered. After winning her fight with eating disorders, she released her first solo album, *Full Circle* at the age of twenty-two. For more information about Halie and her music, visit www.halieloren.com

Heather Purdin, from Boone, NC, is a survivor of an eating disorder and experiences music as a powerful force for healing, a blessing she discovered after buying a guitar during her recovery process. She has a post-master's certificate in expressive arts therapy and will be doing some individual studies soon. Heather also finds time in her busy schedule to go on tour and sing and play keyboards with a reggae/funk band, Selah Dubb. For more information about Heather, and to get in touch with her, visit www.myspace.com/heatherpurdin or www.myspace.com/babybeatsreggae

Holly Elzinga, a twenty-six-year old artist from Chicago, Illinois, struggled with bulimia and finds strong healing power in creating art

J. J. S. is twenty-years old and lives in Pennsylvania. She is a recovering bulimic of eleven years with anorexic tendencies. She is a college student and majors in Human Services with her area of concentration in social work and hopes to become a therapist for eating disorders and give back to people what so many have helped give back to her. If you want to get in touch with her, feel free to send an email to jjs@youarenotalonebook.com

Jana R. L. is in her twenties and lives in Alabama. She is a singer, songwriter and poetry author. She writes about eating disorders as well as many other things she has gone through. Jana has struggled with anorexia and bulimia for many years now, but still sees the light in getting better. "I believe my faith and hope has kept me going this far. I hope my writings can touch and inspire you to see the light through it all!" If you want to get in touch with Jana, feel free to send a message to wjana@bellsouth.net

Jenni Schaefer is a singer/songwriter, speaker, and the author of *Life Without Ed* (McGraw-Hill) and *Goodbye Ed, Hello Me* (McGraw Hill, September 2009). Appointed to the Ambassador Council of the National Eating Disorders Association (NEDA), she is a regular guest on national radio and television. For more information, visit www.jennischaefer.com

Jennifer is thirty-nine years old and lives in the United States. She began her struggle with an eating disorder at the age of thirteen. In spring of 2007, she was admitted to an in-patient treatment facility (Remuda Ranch) for sixty days. She continues to work at recovery and is hopeful that she will finally put this behind her.

Jennifer Friedman, a New York native and graduate of SUNY Purchase, first discovered her love for music as a little girl sitting at her parents' piano. She overcame an eating disorder to record an album of her original songs, and begin performing them. For more information about Jennifer, visit www.jennfriedman.com and www.myspace.com/jennfriedman

Jessica, a twenty-eight-year-old student and writer from Houston, Texas, is recovered from anorexia, bulimia, COE (Compulsive Overeating), self-injury, drug and alcohol abuse, and contributed her recovery story to *You Are Not Alone, Volume I.* Jessica is an eating disorder awareness and prevention actionist and women's issues actionist. For more information, and to get in touch with Jessica, visit www.live-out-loud.org

Jenny Dalton is twenty-nine years old and lives in Minneapolis, Minnesota. She is a singer, pianist, songwriter, and recording artist. Jenny defies pressures to maintain an unhealthy image and nurtures a creative lifestyle through care of the mind, body and soul. For more information about Jenny and her music, visit www.jennydalton.com

Jo is twenty-five years old and lives in England. She struggled with eating disorders for ten years and is now recovered. If you want to get in touch with Jo, feel free to send an email to jo@youarenotalonebook.com

Johnie Drew is twenty-seven years old, married and lives in Tennessee. She has struggled with her eating disorder for twenty years and is now in recovery.

Joy Nollenberg is thirty years old and lives in Minnesota. She struggled with eating disorders for thirteen years and is now recovered. Joy is the founder of *The Joy Project*, a non-profit organization that raises eating disorder awareness. For more information about *The Joy Project* and to get in touch with Joy, go to www.joyproject.org

Linder Dwyer is twenty-three years old and lives in Texas. She struggled with anorexia for one year and with bulimia for four. Now that Linder is recovered, she is experiencing life fully and pursuing her dream of becoming a counselor, and having a good relationship. "I am proof that you can actually get past it!"

Lisa Paige is forty-three years old and lives in Massachusetts. She is in recovery for eating disorders suffered since early childhood. Lisa is currently working on her first poetry book. If you would like to get in touch with Lisa, you can send an email to lisapn@comcast.net

Liz Hardy, a twenty-two-year old college student from the United States, dreams of becoming an English teacher. She is enjoying recovery after struggling with anorexia for eight years. She is a survivor, and that is her first and last thought every morning and night. If you want to get in touch with Liz, feel free to send an email to liz@youarenotalonebook.com

Lori B lives in San Francisco and is a survivor of eating disorders. After a stint in the film business, she trained and practiced as a body-centered psychotherapist in New York City. She has performed and taught various kinds of healing, dancing, music and ritual in theaters and living rooms around the world. For more information about her music, photography, writing and private coaching work, please visit www.loriB.net

Lori Henry is a writer and actor based in Vancouver, Canada. She struggled with bulimia for six years and is now fully recovered. Her book, *Silent Screams* (978-1-4357-1843-2), is a collection of poems written during that time. She was also the publisher and editor of *Beauty: You Define It* magazine. For more information about Lori, visit www.lorihenry.ca

Lucie Beardwood, from Wales (and proud of it!), is a student at the London School of Journalism and is working on her first novel. She currently lives in Gloucestershire, with her two adorable dogs – Deeva the Lhasa Apso and Toby the terror (sorry, Terrier). Lucie struggled with body image issues and disordered eating for many years, culminating in hospitalization and treatment for anorexia. Now that she is recovered, it is her passion to support others in their recovery. She is part of an inspirational eating disorder recovery channel on YouTube (www.youtube.com/user/lifeembracing). If you want to get in touch with Lucie, feel free to send her an email at lucie@youarenotalonebook.com

Lynette Taylor resides in Salt Lake City, UT. She works as a Board-Certified Music Therapist at Center for Change (CFC), an inpatient treatment center for eating disorders. Lynette works to help women find hope in recovery through music. She is also the Director of the CFC

Women's Choir. The song, *My Choice* was written and performed entirely by clients of CFC under Lynette's direction.
For more information about Lynette and the CFC Women's Choir, visit www.centerforchange.com

Mackenzie Brooks, a seventeen-year-old student from Texas, is in recovery from anorexia.

Mary Pat Nally is thirty-eight years old and lives in Ventura County, California. She has her Masters Degree in Spiritual Psychology and has recovered/healed from twenty-four years of eating disordered behaviors. She is the founder of *Learn, Lead and Serve*, whose mission is to provide a space where students of all ages have the opportunity to become their authentic selves. She is a mentor and recovery coach for others who are walking their own healing journey. She is the author of *Reflecting Grace* and is currently working on her second book. Mary Pat is available for speaking and workshop engagements throughout the United States and Canada. For more information and to get in touch with Mary Pat, visit www.authenticallyme.com

Miriam suffered from anorexia. Now that she is recovered, she is enjoying life and the challenges of being a professional scientist. As team leader and editor-in-chief at www.hungrig-online.de, the biggest German website on eating disorders, Miriam is involved every day in supporting and encouraging people struggling with eating disorders.

Patricia Burkley, who is in her sixties and lives in Ohio, graduated from Cleveland Metropolitan General School of Nursing in 1961, where her eating disorder developed into a forty-year obsession. After practicing briefly, she married and left nursing for fourteen years to raise three children. Patricia re-entered nursing, and has been practicing in the psychiatric field since 1990. Finally, aged sixty, she was convinced to enter an eating disorder treatment facility. She collaborated with longtime friend, Dr. Jack Summers, to chronicle her journey to recovery, which resulted in a book entitled *Discovering the Monster Within*. If you want to get in touch with Patricia, feel free to send a message to ajburkley@aol.com

Reema Arora is a medical student living in Chicago, Illinois.

Regina Edgar is twenty-three years old and lives in Michigan. She is recovered from a ten-year battle with anorexia. She also recovered from a six-year struggle with self-injury and is a sexual abuse and rape survivor. Regina is a co-writer for *One Life*, a website dedicated to recovery from eating disorders and self-injury (www.river-tree.net/onelife/). If you want to get in touch with Regina, feel free to send her an email at youngfiddler@hotmail.com

Robin Maynard-Dobbs is a personal coach and founder of *Aware Eating*. She has been helping women successfully overcome compulsive eating since 1991. Robin offers a unique and holistic approach to recovery from eating disorders and obsession with food / weight. Through mindfulness, Robin guides women to connect and respond to their bodies with kindness. As women let go of judgment, they learn how to eat naturally, and to care for their bodies with honor and respect. For many years, Robin was driven by compulsive overeating followed by excessive exercise so she knows firsthand the process of recovery from an eating disorder. As she now lives in joy and harmony with her body, she is freed up to pursue her passion of helping other women overcome their struggle with food. Inspired by a lifelong meditation practice, she teaches others to look inside themselves for the wisdom they seek. Based in Seattle, Washington, Robin is available either in person or coaching over the phone. For more information about Robin and her work and to sign up for a free half hour initial consultation, visit www.awareeating.com

Robin Richardson, from Boulder, Colorado, is recovering from anorexia, bulimia, and alcoholism. She is also an incest survivor who is now thriving in her life. A singer-songwriter and inspirational speaker for all age groups, Robin is also a psychotherapist working with disordered eating, sexual abuse, and addictions. Robin's newest CD, *Wild Bird*, chronicles her journey out of addiction and despair into peace, self-love, and a life worth living. *Wild Bird* is available on www.sunlightofthespirit.com. For more information about Robin, visit www.robinrichardson.net

Shannon Cutts is the author of *Beating Ana: How to Outsmart Your Eating Disorder and Take Your Life Back* (Health Communications, Inc.) and founder of Key to Life: unlocking the door to hope, an organization that provides programs, workshops, concerts, products, and services to foster awareness, education, intervention, and prevention of eating and related disorders. More recently, Shannon founded MentorCONNECT, the first global mentoring network to connect those in strong recovery from eating disorders with those who need recovery support. For more information about Shannon and her work, visit www.key-to-life.com

Theresa Grimsley is thirty-three years old and lives in the United States. Theresa is married and has two sons. She struggled with anorexia and bulimia for over fifteen years and is now in recovery.

Tricia Fowler is in recovery from anorexia and bulimia. If you want to get in touch with Tricia, feel free to send an email to giraffe_lover_forever@hotmail.com

Whitney Greenwood is a twenty-one year old, multi-racial (minorities get eating disorders too), student from the United States. She recovered from bulimia, anorexia, occasional self-injury, and suicidal tendencies. She also struggled with Attention Deficit Hyperactivity Disorder, and is in recovery from a mood disorder and anxiety.

Additional Resources

Eating Disorder Support Resources:

Something Fishy (www.somethingfishy.org)
Something-Fishy provides information on all forms of eating disorders, related topics, plus much more, and most important of all, it provides support to everyone affected by eating disorders, and their loved-ones.

Pale Reflections (www.pale-reflections.com)
Pale Reflections is an online community for everyone affected by eating disorders and provides information on all forms of eating disorders, depression, obsessive compulsive disorder, and much more.

Eating Disorder Referral (www.edreferral.com)
EDReferral.com provides information and treatment resources for all forms of eating disorders. This site provides assistance in the form of information and resources to those suffering with eating disorders to get them started on the road to recovery and healthy living.

Gürze Books (www.gurze.com)
Bulimia.com specializes in information about eating disorders including Anorexia, Bulimia, and Binge Eating Disorder, plus related topics such as Body Image and Obesity. This website offers eating disorder books at discounted prices, articles about eating disorders, newsletters, and links to treatment facilities, organizations, other websites, and much more.

Self-Harm Support Resources:

RecoverYourLife.com (www.recoveryourlife.com)
RecoverYourLife.com is one of the biggest and best self-harm communities on the Internet. Communicate with other members and realize you are not alone. Whether you want help in reducing or stopping your self-harm, or you just aren't ready yet, everyone is welcome here.

RecoverYourLife's members have proved many thousands of times that self-harm can be beaten and that there is hope.

LifeSIGNS (www.selfharm.org)
LifeSIGNS is a voluntary organization that raises awareness about the syndrome of self-injury in the UK and beyond. LifeSIGNS provides much needed information and training to organizations; offering unique services not available from any other voluntary organizations.

S.A.F.E. Alternatives (www.safe-alternatives.com and www.selfinjury.com)
S.A.F.E. Alternatives (Self-Abuse Finally Ends) is a nationally recognized treatment approach, professional network and educational resource base which is committed to helping you and others achieve an end to self-injurious behavior.

Sexual Abuse and Rape Support Resources:

Broken Spirits (www.brokenspirits.com)
Broken Spirits is an online community and support group that focuses on aiding both current and past victims of child abuse, sexual abuse, and domestic violence. This website is an interactive, personal support website dedicated to helping each other through the pain and fear of an abusive relationship. It provides a comprehensive International Directory of shelters, hotlines and organizations that can provide help for potential victims. In addition to the national abuse resource listing there is a comprehensive discussion forum where users can create their own virtual identity with complete confidentiality.

After Silence (www.aftersilence.org)
After Silence is a community designed website to help survivors communicate in their recovery from rape and sexual abuse; and to support, empower, validate, and educate survivors of rape and sexual abuse, as well as secondary survivors. The core of this website is a community where survivors come together online in a mutually supportive environment.

Whitedove's Nest (www.whitedovesnest.com)
Whitedove's Nest is dedicated to survivors of sexual abuse and those who support them. It provides information on sexual abuse, personal stories,

articles, inspiration and help to those affected by sexual abuse, rape, and molestation.

The Rape, Abuse & Incest National Network (www.rainn.org)
The Rape, Abuse & Incest National Network (RAINN) is the nation's largest anti-sexual assault organization. Among its programs, RAINN created and operates the National Sexual Assault Hotline at 1.800.656.HOPE. This nationwide partnership of more than 1,100 local rape treatment hotlines provides victims of sexual assault with free, confidential services around the clock.

You Are Invited To Join The ***You Are Not Alone SUPPORT LETTER Community!***

Dear Friend,

Every month, I send out a special email newsletter filled with personal recovery stories, inspirational sayings, special guest interviews with eating disorder experts, speakers and survivors, useful tips, inspiring poems and artwork, healing information, and much more. Here is just a sample of what is shared:

- An international model opens up about her struggles with, and ultimate victory over, bulimia, and what she is doing now to help others and raise awareness.
- How one girl used the Tyra Banks show to learn to love her body.
- A Hollywood actress talks about her battle with, and recovery from, anorexia, and what she is doing now to help others in their recovery.
- Thirty-three recovery projects to help you on your healing journey.
- "I am finally beginning to live again!" – One Support Letter reader shares her story.
- Learning to love the way you look – Three key things that helped me overcome my body image issues.
- A former male model opens up about his struggle with binge eating disorder and how he managed to recover.
- How to survive the holidays – Tips and tricks on how to make the best out of the holiday season!
- "I am me. Not my eating disorder." – One Support Letter reader opens up.
- How one woman from England fully recovered from her seven-year battle with eating disorders.
- Give-aways.
- And much more.

It is a completely free newsletter.

Simply go to www.youarenotalonebook.com/supportletter.html to reserve your subscription.

All the best to you, and continue to be strong!

Andrea Roe

PS. You have read the book. Now connect to the community that made this project possible in the first place. Join the *You Are Not Alone Support Letter* community at www.youarenotalonebook.com/supportletter.html

PPS. Here is what readers are saying about the Support Letter:

"*The You Are Not Alone Support Letter* and Andrea – the one behind it all – are truly a blessing that has come into my life. She has put so much into this work, which does not stop at that – her generosity, knowledge, and personal support and encouragement have helped me through tough times since I found this site. I can personally attest to the fact that she does care and wants ALL of US to recover and will lend a hand, give advice, and offer a shoulder when times are tough. Thank you, Andrea, for all your time, effort, knowledge, and support you continue to give to touch others. You have truly touched and helped me during my recovery."

– Emily, from Tennessee, has battled anorexia for nine years

"I had anorexia for ten years, but I am recovered now and this website (www.youarenotalonebook.com) absolutely helped me a lot. Although I am recovered, I still read every issue of the Support Letter and look forward every month to the latest edition."

– Aylicia from Singapore recovered from eating disorders

"I really do enjoy the Support Letter. I recommended it to my nutritionist because I think so much of the information and so many of the tips are extremely helpful, and I hope that she will be able to pass on some of your compassion and information to others with eating disorders (she works at the Renfrew Center in CT). My favorite parts of the newsletter are the tips sections (how to survive the holidays), the inspirational quotes, the thoughts by celebrities (because for me the media plays a large part in my body image issues and anorexia), and the personal story. I think the whole newsletter is extremely well put together. The history information is pretty cool to read about and putting a different personal story in each newsletter is inspiring. I just wanted to say that I am grateful for all your hard work in putting this newsletter together. It gives me the extra hope to continue to heal."

– Elissa struggled with anorexia, depression and anxiety for about twelve years